DECORATING

With Laurence Llewelyn-Bowen

DECORATING

With Laurence Llewelyn-Bowen

Quadrille
PUBLISHING

The author and publisher take no responsibility for any injury or loss arising from the procedures or materials described in this book. Materials, tools, skills and work areas vary greatly and are the responsibility of the reader. Always follow the manufacturer's instructions and take the appropriate safety precautions.

Editorial Director *Anne Furniss*
Creative Director *Helen Lewis*
Art Director *Gabriella Le Grazie*
Design Concept *Llewelyn-Bowen Limited*
Project Editor *Simon Davis*
Photography *Polly Wreford, Carolyn Barber*
Production *Vincent Smith, Marina Asenjo*
Editorial Assistant *Sarah Jones*

First published in 2010 by
Quadrille Publishing Limited
Alhambra House, 27-31 Charing Cross Road,
London WC2H 0LS
www.quadrille.co.uk

Text © 2010 Laurence Llewelyn-Bowen
Photography © 2010 Quadrille Publishing Limited
Design and layout © 2010 Quadrille Publishing Limited

Cataloguing-in-Publication Data: a catalogue record for this book is available from the British Library.

ISBN 978 184400 814 8 (UK trade edition)
ISBN 978 184400 877 3 (Export edition)

Printed in China

CONTENTS

BEING YOUR OWN INTERIOR DESIGNER

DIY doesn't just stand for 'do it yourself'; it can also mean 'design it yourself'. This is where the real fun comes in, giving you the opportunity to really make your mark on a space.

CREATING A DESIGN SCHEME

When people ask me where they should start designing their room, I often suggest they begin with a cold glass of chardonnay. Though this advice may sound flippant, there is a point to it – at this first stage of the design process it is important that you are as relaxed and as unconstrained as possible. Spend time building up a mental picture of your own fantasy room; the more a scheme gets thought through, the better it becomes. By the time I hit the drawing board, I like to feel that the whole thing has been more or less entirely thought through in my head.

To create your dream room you will need to assemble some inspiration. At this stage, try to keep it as broad as possible. If something appeals, then photograph it or tear it out of a magazine. A fridge, a colour, a tropical island, or a pattern on a couture frock – some of the most unexpected things can provide you with that potentially highly creative starting point.

Once you have assembled images for what is known in the trade as a 'mood board', put them together on a piece of card. The images don't need to be arranged in orderly fashion, the point is to see whether any particular combination of images stands out. You may well find that one image next to a picture of something completely different suddenly inspires that spark of inspiration and, hey presto, a creative idea is born.

Now start collating that creative freedom into something more structured. With your empty room firmly fixed in your mind, try painting it in imaginary colours with imaginary treatments for the walls. Play around with different floor ideas. All the while you should keep relating back to your mood board for inspiration.

GO SHOPPING

Well, at least go window shopping. Narrow down your choices to specific products. Start collating a visual presentation with samples and photographs of specific items. Keep your search broad – you do not have to be overly practical whilst you have your creative hat on, so don't drop that sofa just because of its king's-ransom-sized price tag. At this stage stay as loyal as you can to the creative idea. The budget will have its sway later, but not just yet.

WRITE A TO-DO LIST

Write a list of what needs to be done. Start with the big stuff like building work or major interior carpentry, then make headings to include all the other bits and pieces – plumbing, electrics, flooring, decorating, soft furnishings, upholstery and the fabulous 'FFF' (furniture, fittings and furnishing). Though it may not sound enthralling, there is a lot of pleasure to be had in getting this list right. Try to keep the proposed scheme at the front of your mind as you start imagining the new elements in your blank canvas room arriving one by one. As you do, check everything is in the right place: if you want to put the television in that corner, is there an aerial point and a wall socket nearby? If you put the sofa under that window, will it block the view or, more positively, will it hide that radiator?

WORK UP YOUR DESIGN PRESENTATION

As your choices become more finely honed, start working up the level of detail in your design scheme. Your design presentation should now have a sample or a picture of everything you are planning to do. For every product that you have chosen for your room, your presentation should include as much detail as possible. So, where your list says paint the ceiling, list the paint and put in details of the supplier; where it says lay the carpet, give all the necessary reference numbers to ensure the right carpet arrives.

BUDGETING

Now tot up your budget – yes, the scary bit. The reason you've been so solicitous with your design presentation is so that, should you suddenly decide you cannot afford it all at once, then at least you have a fixed design goal to aim for as you implement the elements piecemeal. Your considered presentation will also help keep your confidence levels up as you go through the process of transforming your room. One of the worst things you could ever do is to run out of steam halfway through and suddenly decide that the wall colour's too dark or that the carpets are too frantically patterned. Always remember that all the elements are there to work in combination, as a team. Singly and out of context they may very well seem incoherent, but when balanced by all the ingredients in your presentation they will be just what the room needs.

And, even when the budget manages to break its own boundaries, try to keep the ideas contained within your design presentation sacrosanct. So, if the original sofa with its luxurious fabric is way too expensive, perhaps a plainer cheaper sofa with a few big cushions in the same fabric could achieve the same effect? That wallpaper that you have chosen may cost the earth, but have you thought about rolling up your sleeves and making something similar yourself with a stencil? I can honestly say that creativity can get you out of some seemingly insurmountable budgeting tight spots – as long as you have a detailed design presentation to work from you will be fine.

Practical design

I resent interiors that turn their owners into slaves. What looks jawdropping in a glossy interiors magazine may very well, in everyday life, require a fleet of house servants to maintain. It is also worth remembering that nothing opts out of getting old: it is called entropy and is inescapable. A sensible mindset then is to focus on design schemes that get old gracefully.

Choose easy to clean (or at least easy to change) Large expanses of glass may seem marvellously modern but they will need a lot of elbow grease to keep them looking good. When choosing paint, remember that easily repainted emulsion is often a more practical solution than difficult-to-apply gloss.

Go mid-tone As very dark or very light colours show age far worse than mid-tone shades.

Camouflage wear and tear Pattern is a great way of distracting the eye away from damage.

Choose darker flooring Floor coverings start 'shadowing' after a few years of use, so work out where the most trafficked areas are and choose dark or mid-tone shades accordingly.

Ventilate Keep bathroom and kitchens well-ventilated to prevent finishes being assailed by damp.

SPACE

It is very rare to meet someone who feels that their home is the perfect size. Often they will have a long list of gripes about it. There are too few bedrooms; the kitchen isn't big enough to swing a smallish cat; or the children don't have the space they need to run around inside when it rains, for example.

And yet, for all these complaints relating to size, in my experience it is the aesthetics of the home that will often tip the balance from 'house love' to 'house hate'. While we can usually accommodate the practically imperfect, we are far harder on those spaces that, just by looking at them, give that overwhelming yet intangible feeling of gloomy depression. The architectural personality of a room has a powerful but often unremarked influence on one's state of mind. Our eye might get snagged on the fripperies – the colours, the details, and the furniture – but ultimately if the room feels wrong, we all feel wrong. Yet admitting that a room is fundamentally the wrong shape sounds terminal; without full-scale architectural remodelling surely the space is a write-off?

Not so. Just as clever dressing can distract the eye from a long list of bodily imperfections, so interior decoration has some wonderfully clever tricks up its wizard's sleeve of makeover.

CUTTING CORNERS

Luckily for us decorators, the human eye has a very turbulent relationship with the brain, which (bless it) is prone to making mistakes when assessing space. From experience the brain knows that to get a handle on the space it is in it needs to know where the corners are, so it sends a message to the eye to find the darkish upright lines it has come to trust as being the visual signposts to the perimeter. If the eye cannot find these signposts, then the brain sloppily assumes the room is much bigger. And that, ladies and gentleman, is the single most important thing you need to remember!

So, given that your room is likely to come complete with corners (and that you are very unlikely to be able to remove them), what is to be done? The best way to make those corners disappear is by making an eye-catching fuss of the space between them. The magpie brain cannot help but be captivated by this, trapped in the middle and blithely uninterested in the edges. This most simple and effective of decorating tricks does not just apply to walls – floor space can also be made to feel far more generous by painting the skirting the same colour as the floor, while the installation of an eye-catching statement chandelier will transform your ceiling into an immense tundra of uninhabited space.

USING STRIPES TO STRETCH A SPACE

It may or may not surprise you to learn that the 'vertical lines elongate, horizontal lines broaden' rule that we all apply to ourselves when dressing also relates to the proportions of our rooms. The key to making short, dumpy rooms feel tall and willowy is to remember to sprinkle verticals such as full-length curtains, long thin panels or even graciously leggy standard lamps wherever you can. Not only do these upright lines help stretch the room's proportions vertically, their sheer number also catches the eye and makes those annoying corners even more difficult to spot. Likewise, when used cleverly in a room, broad horizontal emphasis can makes a space appear twice the width it really is.

Room layouts

Getting the layout of a room right is a careful balance between practicality and aesthetics. Personally, I like a room to both look sensational and be convenient which, for me, means that everything has a preordained place where it works best.

LIVING ROOMS

L-shaped works best These days so many of our living rooms convene around the television. Often the principal visual axis runs straight from the most comfortable sofa to the TV screen, which can be difficult in rooms originally built around the warm amber glow of the fireplace. Modern solutions involving major architectural intrusion are all well and good, but the simplest solution is to create an L-shaped seating arrangement – with one sofa favouring the fireplace and another favouring the television.

BEDROOMS

Don't be a wallflower There's always space for a little creativity when it comes to bedroom layouts, so don't feel tied to the walls. If there's room, putting the bed in the middle of the space can look very grand. Make sure there is a headboard so that the pillows don't keep falling off the end and consider a piece of furniture like a console table or desk at the foot of the bed to finish the whole thing off.

KITCHENS

Put the home into home kitchen An unloved haven for the cook to slave away in a hundred years ago, these days the kitchen is an incredibly important room that must be the kind of space in which we can live as well as cook. I love kitchens that feel integrated into the rest of the home – with lamps on the work surfaces for gentle mood lighting, and pictures and wallpaper on the walls. If at all possible, I try also to avoid wall-hung cupboards, which always feel heavy and create a claustrophobic effect. I know you've got to keep them tidy, but using open shelves in place of wall-hung cupboards dramatically increases the feeling of space and light within a room.

RHYTHM AND CONTRAST

Once you have opened up the box of interior tricks and have transformed some of those spatial wrongs into proportional rights, your room will need a bit of finessing. A bit of civilising, if you like. You'll also want to create emphasis in certain places, to generate interest and make features out of particular elements within a room. To achieve both these goals, an understanding of the concepts of rhythm and contrast is essential.

RHYTHM

When you see pictures of extraordinary beautiful rooms from the past, one of the key ingredients of their glamour is one of the most difficult things to spot. Unless, that is, you know where to look. Rhythm has a huge influence on interiors but, when it is done properly, it becomes more or less entirely invisible.

We like rhythm – it is good for the soul. Neurological experiments have proved time and again that measured elegant rhythm spreads waves of pleasure through the brain. It is as if we love to know what's coming next: left, right, left, right, left (and isn't it wonderful to feel safe in the knowledge that right comes next?). We like the security of understanding past, present, then future; which is why wall, curtain, window, curtain, wall, curtain, window, curtain breeds a sense of comfortable familiarity.

SYMMETRY AND BALANCE

Rhythm at its simplest and most efficient, symmetry delights us. We see ourselves as symmetrical and love it when our environments reflect our proportions.

Arrangements of pairs, using twos, fours or eights all create a pleasant sense of visual harmony. The danger with a space that is too symmetrical, however, is that it can easily degenerate into a space without energy. By contrast the asymmetrical forces an instant reaction from us – if symmetry lulls us into a sense of soft-focus security, then a lack of symmetry can wake us up with a bang.

So, is there, out there, a midpoint between the sensible, ordered world of the symmetrical and the wild pagan bacchanalia of modernist asymmetry? There is, and it is called balance. Using different objects to balance either side of an invisible centre line is a best-of-both-worlds alternative. As an exercise, it requires everything to be seen in terms of visual weight: the more eye-catching an object, the heavier it is. So a particular 'look-at-me' fireplace in shiny aluminium would need several much smaller framed prints hung as a unit opposite to create equilibrium.

CONTRAST

Contrast livens up a space, but how do you go about bringing it into your scheme? First, select the element of your room that you would like to make a feature of. Then treat it in the opposite way to its neighbours. So, if you want the eye to be immediately drawn to a centrally placed chimney breast, why not wallpaper it? Or should you want to make a huge fuss of one shiny wall, why not try surrounding it with three matt walls? Colour can also be a very effective way of providing contrast; while a beige suede sofa standing on a beige fitted carpet has little impact, making that sofa a shiny red patent creates contrast and makes for a far more theatrical statement.

The feature wall

The concept of contrast is best seen in the use of the feature wall. Painting, papering or treating one wall in a way that is more eye-catching than its three neighbours became popular in the 1950s, with rationing still in force. One wall could be papered using two rolls of wallpaper rather than the eight it would have taken to cover the whole room. As a result, and since invention is indeed the sister of expedience, this quickly became the 'look'.

Choosing the right wall Feature walls can carry a heavy price; if got wrong they can totally overbalance a once-pleasant room. The optical science behind the feature wall theory is pretty straightforward – make one wall so eye-catching that the other three recede into the never-ever. But choose the wrong wall at your peril! In a long narrow room the end wall, the wall furthest from you, is an ideal case for the feature wall. Treated differently it will march bombastically forward, squaring off the space and killing off the room's corridor-like proportions. But should you do the same to one of the side walls, or worse still both of them, the room will become a vice. Bringing walls forward at the room's narrowest point in this way is a work of true folly.

COLOUR

If architecture is the intellect of a room, then colour is its emotion. It is also the first thing we notice about any interior. We have all got favourite colours (and indeed least favourite colours) and none of us can look at a colour without it unleashing all sorts of wonderful prejudices and preconceptions.

All of this makes inheriting somebody else's colour scheme far more difficult than being left with their interior layout. It also makes the act of choosing colours a little bit like walking through an imaginary minefield - with bad taste set to blow up in your face at any moment. So how should you begin? The good news is that colours are less fashionable than they used to be. There was a time when the 'taste makers' would decree a particular shade as 'in', thereby ensuring any other colour was 'out'. With the democratisation of taste, there is no-one to say that you cannot have a lilac bedroom or a brown sitting room, should you wish. While trends in colour do still exist (and flicking through this book it occurred to me that I certainly have a favourite palette that crops up a lot), as a professional interior designer I think it's really important that the lid to the paint box stays open, and that colours I may have dismissed in the past get given a second chance if they suit the room and the client.

COMBINING COLOURS

An ability to put colours together is often treated with mystical awe. While putting colours next to one another is not easy (and isn't helped by the fact that colour is so subjective) there are a few lessons that help. One of the most basic is the kindergarten concept of complementary colours. On the colour wheel, if you remember, there are three primary colours - red, blue and yellow. From these a group of secondary colours are created by mixing – green, orange and purple. And then, spreading out like a very colourful snowflake, infinite combinations create infinite colours. Pinks, turquoises, browns, greys, terracottas - all the shades that you could possibly imagine.

When it comes to complementary colours, opposites attract - repulsively or attractively depending on your point of view. Putting green next to red will intensify both, creating an energetic crescendo of colour. If you are a real colourphile then remember – fortune favours the brave! Societies like those of southern India, where colour is highly valued, use a number of these high-octane primary colour combinations; red and green, blue and yellow and purple and orange. Likewise the Victorians loved to squeeze every last atom out of colour – as shown by the red and green combinations which they used to breathe new life into the Scottish tartan industry.

COLOURS THAT GO

I cannot bear it when people say that colours 'go'. It's not just a case of semantics; I think it puts people in completely the wrong frame of mind; leading them to expect a colour scheme to somehow energetically propel itself towards them. Instead, I prefer to say that colours 'rhyme'. This implies a colour relationship that has a subtle and subjective ability to grow more attractive through familiarity, rather than the definitive 'yes' or 'no' implied by 'go'. One exercise that really helps when it comes to finding colours which co-exist well is to stop thinking of them purely visually and to start transposing them into other senses instead. Though it may sound strange, imagining colours as flavours (citrus-y limes and

yellows for example) can really help to give you a fresh new perspective on colour choice and is a technique that I have often found to be very successful.

STUCK IN NEUTRAL

The late-twentieth century was definitively the age of beige. Before then, noone would have dreamt of using such a colourless colour. Beige and all its neutral friends - taupe, string, straw, magnolia and white chocolate - suited the mood of a new, energetically democratic era that was extremely self-conscious about taste and class. Somehow neutrals showed you to be, well, neutral: neither fish nor fowl, neither pretentiously posh nor aggressively oikish. My sincere hope is that as we all grow in confidence we can start to explore and enjoy colour again, if for no other reason than because getting a beige colour scheme to work is horrendously difficult. All too often I have seen colour schemes that end up as clashing mushes of euphemistic neutrals. Though beige and taupe might seem politely quiet, they can actually clash very noisily indeed.

COLOUR AND DISTANCE

Next time you're in an art gallery, go and have a very close-up look at an Impressionist painting. There are just two things you have to remember about the Impressionists – they painted *en plein aire* (i.e. outside in front of the thing they wanted to paint), and they never used black. So, just how did they get that sense of distance into their wonderful landscapes? Well, rather than using tone, they used hue. They noticed that if they painted far distant mountains blue, grey, lilac, or even sometimes pink, and used reds, browns and dark purples in the foreground, for example, they were able to achieve a pronounced sense of recession; those mountains really did seem much further away.

If cool colours can make painted mountains feel further away, then it only takes a small logical leap to realise that the same shades can help make the walls of your room feel that little bit more distant. In contrast, reds, browns, deep oranges and purples can create that warm, cosy, enclosed effect as they bring the walls further into the space.

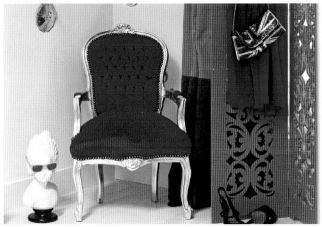

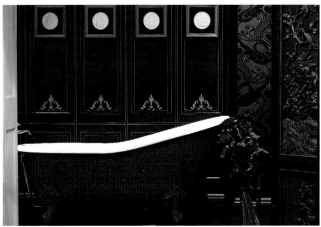

PATTERN

Until recently, pattern has been seen as something of a naughty pleasure by many. All those serious interior designers who peddled schemes of unhindered minimalism and clean-surfaced restraint viewed the voluptuous delights of pattern with horror.

Like colour, pattern comes with stories and associations that mean it always has a lot to say in a room. Large, full-blown, floral patterns conjure up suggestions of traditional decorating and old-fashioned values. Imperialistic, abstract, organic patterns like damasks can go either way: to some they mean history, royalty and richness; to others they'll forever be associated with tacky flock wallpaper and over-decorated 1960's boudoirs. Stripes and plaid, by contrast, carry the gentlemanly whiff of old school tie, preppy rectitude or, failing that, Jane Austen primness.

As with selecting colours, choosing patterns will therefore always be personal and, personally, I like to research a pattern before committing to it. I like to know where it's from and how it was used so that I can really get under its skin. I find it helps when putting things together for a scheme to understand that a particular pattern has its roots in, say, Persian pattern-making tradition. With this in mind I will then search out further elements from the same origin or with the same design inspiration, which I will then introduce into the space where possible.

Using pattern

Repeat a pattern 5 times From experience, I have always found very small-scale close-repeating patterns difficult to pull off in a design scheme. From a distance they tend to merge and become a bit of a mushy visual puddle. Be it wallpapers blinds or curtains, in an ideal world a good rule of thumb is to choose a pattern where a repeated motif can fit roughly five times vertically in the room. Any smaller and I think you run the risk of busyness, any larger and it'll feel incomplete.

More is often more Just as a highly edited, minimalist room takes twice the budget, effort and maintenance of a more maximalist scheme, so an outrageously joyful application of pattern on pattern provides more distraction and stimulation than a scheme conceived around one repeat. Putting patterns together does take a confident decisive eye - not only do the colours used need to be balanced, there are motifs and repeats that also require consideration. Weirdly though, I find that the more patterns that are used within a space, the easier this is to pull off.

Apply to all four walls to maximise space Pattern provides us with a very important weapon in the war against small-scale space. Just as camouflage on a tank is there to confuse the eye and blur the outline, so the right sort of wallpaper (i.e. a paper with a strong contrast and non-geometric pattern) is the best room camouflage that money can buy. Run over all four walls it does a brilliant vanishing act with the room's corners, while big, heavy bits of architecture like chimney breasts, cumbersome cupboards or clumsily placed doors can also be made to melt away in a haze of wallpaper pattern.

LIGHTING

The relentless advance of technology has meant that something as simple as lighting a room has now become very complicated. As far as I am concerned, lighting in the home is simple if you remember the three golden rules: use lots of it, place it low and illuminate up. Lighting the perimeter of a room is a good place to start; deliberately placing lamps in the corners of a room is a clever way of blurring its edges and increasing the overall sense of space. Likewise, placing lamps on low tables helps send light upwards, intensifying a feeling of glowing enclosure and making the most of the room's vertical space. Whatever else you do, avoid having just the one strong, centrally placed light source. Though this may work well in a morgue, it's a disaster in a domestic setting – casting highlights and shadows that will make everything and everyone look unbelievably ugly.

CREATING A LIGHTING SCHEME

While having light where you need it is extremely important, working out where that lighting should go is always so much easier on paper. Drawing up a lighting scheme is a great opportunity to explore the different lighting possibilities that exist, with the added result being that a neat, finalised plan (if it results in the need for rewiring) can also be used by an electrician as a guide. Remember that, for large rooms and open plan spaces in particular, it's very important that a lighting scheme takes into account the whole area. There is no point in planning the lighting for the dining area of a living room, say, without considering the impact that this will have on the rest of the space, as it will just end up an incoherent mess.

Though it can be expensive, rewiring a room will mean that the power sources for your lighting will be exactly where they are needed. The result is not only more aesthetically pleasing and safer – as you won't need miles of ugly, dangerous trailing cable in order to plug your light into the nearest wall socket – it can also make life far more convenient. If I am having a room rewired, I will often opt for a 5 amp circuit, which means that tall lamps on 5 amp circuits can be switched on or off from one point. So, no more having to jump up and down to switch each lamp off or on individually and no need to get out of bed to turn off all the lights in a room. What could be better?

TYPES OF LIGHTING

While it's true that there are many flavours of light, as long as you can understand the differences between them you will be able to choose the light that is best suited to your space with confidence.

INCANDESCENT BULBS

Most homes are lit by traditional incandescent bulbs which give a reliable, warm glow. Their effect can be varied by strength as in wattage, or by the bulb itself being sprayed with an opaque pearlescent finish or even a colour coating.

HALOGEN BULBS

Down lights, spotlights and many contemporary lamps use halogen. Halogen gives off a very clean, pure light and as such is used widely in shops to really show a product off to its best advantage. Its effect isn't a million miles away from daylight, so it is great in very dark areas that have to be entirely artificially lit.

ENERGY-SAVING BULBS

Energy-saving light bulbs are extremely difficult to work with. Like the fluorescent tube (to which they are closely related), the light they give has plenty of illumination, but little romance or subtlety. Energy-saving bulbs are best used inside strongly coloured glass light fittings. If they are used in a conventional lamp base, I find a foil-lined lampshade in old gold or bronze to be the only way of counteracting their ugly, milky glow.

FLUORESCENT BULBS

Whilst being energy efficient and useful for fridges, fluorescent lighting has no subtlety whatsoever. Its strong, blue characteristic has a habit of sucking any warmth out of any interior it illuminates.

Using reflected light

Loving nothing more than to boisterously bounce from shiny surfaces, reflected light helps in making a space feel lively and interesting. Furniture buffed to a highy polished sheen, light-reflecting silky or glazed fabrics, and lustrous foil wallpapers all do marvellous work at helping out daylight, while the following options can transform your room from dim to dazzling.

Lay reflective flooring While fitted carpets are a wonderful, voluptuous treat for the eyes and feet, they do gobble up daylight. Hard floor surfaces like wood, marble or vinyl by contrast reflect light magnificently. What few people realise, however, is that they do this job far better the darker they are.

Choose leggy furniture There is no point in having all that light-reflecting potential on the floor if your room is choked up with heavy furniture – anything soft or absorbent will stop it dead in its tracks. Instead, go for leggy furniture which will increase the sense of both light and space.

Use art to light the way Whilst not quite so obvious, I have often found that art can make a surprising difference to the light levels of a room. In very dark rooms, I'll often use pictures with deliberately over-generous pale ivory mounts and narrow gold leaf frames to help break up the gloom and act as regularly spaced light reflectors.

Experiment with mirrors Mirrors reflect space, light, and shade and, used properly, can glam up any interior. For those that fear their own reflection might prove to be (over time) too distracting, try placing a picture in front of the mirror itself at eye level. This means that the mirror does what it's there for and reflects the room without you constantly catching your own eye. And don't just see mirrors as living only on walls. Pieces of mirror cut to size and used on specific bits of furniture can reflect light brilliantly.

UTILITIES

For me there is no sense in denying the existence of twenty-first-century utilities and conveniences. Even in historical interiors (in fact often especially in historical interiors) I like to use technology in unashamedly head-on fashion. Indeed, provided they are properly and elegantly designed, there can often be a real design advantage to be gained from using a sprinkle of contemporary elements within a scheme.

TELEVISIONS

Since the advent of the flat screen, the television is no longer the bullying, hulking presence it once was. I like to put televisions in busy contexts where there is a lot going on, so that the screen is not necessarily the first thing you see. On shelves or in bookcases, televisions become part of a much larger display and, as a result, are far less dominant. Their impact can also be lessened by integrating their black screens into a colour scheme - perhaps by placing them next to a dark picture or a run of black-spined books. And if you do find their presence unbearably overwhelming, you can always try storing them in cupboards or behind doors.

SWITCHES AND SOCKETS

Now that switches and sockets come in designed finishes such as slate, copper, glass, chrome or brass, I like to see them as accents – with their position on a wall and their relationship with all other elements within the room carefully considered. Where wallpaper is the hero of the scheme, subtle acrylic panelled switches that let the paper show through have a lot going for them, for example.

RADIATORS

Like electrical switches and sockets, radiators now come as design statements in their own right. Provided they have been properly integrated into a scheme and their inclusion has been thoroughly thought through, I really do not object to seeing radiators. Putting a shelf over a radiator is an idea that I am very keen on. From a practical perspective, this helps to redirect heat efficiently back into the room as well as reducing heat damage to the wall, whilst aesthetically it creates an opportunity for displaying eye-catching 'still lives' that can distract attention away from the radiator below. If, however, you do want to minimise a radiator's visual impact, try either painting it to blend in with a wall or render it invisible by placing it behind an open-back bookcase or sofa, from where it will function perfectly happily.

Storage

While there are obviously going to be some things in life that don't get used everyday, to be honest I find myself at a loss when faced with the current obsession with 'storage'. It is all part and parcel of minimalism, I suppose...though any minimalist statement fails dismally if, rather than reducing your life to an essential essence, it merely sweeps it under the carpet. My general feeling is that if you have got stuff that cannot be put on display, then why have it in the first place?

Store in plain sight I admit I am a maximalist. I love to be surrounded by objects I own that give me pleasure. I love the combinations and relationships they strike up and I love being able to relive the experiences that accompany them. Generally speaking, then, wherever I can I like to use chunky open shelves on which books, lamps, televisions, plants, flowers and clutter all jostle for good-natured attention.

Integrate storage into your design scheme
Of course, not everything you own can be out on display. Even I would baulk at a shelf displaying an inflatable dinghy, several Christmas napkins and a toolbox. So a degree of storage will always be necessary; and, where you do need it, try to incorporate it into your design scheme as early as possible. If conceived at an early-enough stage in the development of your room, cupboards, buckets and boxes can work within the architectural layout of a space and provide you with all the practical storage solutions you need, while remaining neat and discrete.

ROOMS TO INSPIRE

WALLPAPER CUT TO SHAPE

BED SIDE ON

PARENTAL RETREAT

WARDROBE DOORS

TV

Baroque 'n' roll

Modern design doesn't have to hold back on the glam. Riding the revival of interest in all things rich, this urban pad blings very brightly indeed.

On paper the tartan carpet, the gold trellis paper, the ornate bed head and the wall of postcards shouldn't really work. Sure, they are bits and pieces from many different sources but they all sit more than happily in the same scheme because they are all based on grid patterns. I was inspired by the gritty urban detailing of the gridded balcony fronts that dominate the foreground of the formerly industrialised cityscape beyond the window of this modern urban flat. I loved the idea of taking something so aggressively anti-decorative and using it as a starting point for what has proved to be an incredibly indulgent visual feast. But all along I've kept an eye on context and there's nothing about this space that denies its contemporary architectural style. Even the bare concrete ceiling has a part to play in ensuring that this room keeps a particularly rock and roll flavoured edge to it. Black and gold has been a high-calorie colour combination. It's a very, very naughty story and one which relies on the fact that each colour brings out quite the most attention-grabbing behaviours in the other. Against black, gold becomes a beacon of indulgence and on gold, black is transformed into a dense, sulking shadow. This scheme is a perfect example of the sort of high-risk, high-return decorating I love. It was only when the last few elements arrived that the room suddenly started to work, proving how finely balanced the success of this sort of look actually is.

1

Art attack

This ever-changing wall of postcards from the Tate galleries is a wonderful way of furnishing a workstation corner. Images can be added or subtracted depending on inspiration. I grudgingly suppose that lists, timetables, schedules or pizza delivery leaflets could also feature...if they had to. The console tables were made very simply from MDF which was then covered in Anaglypta, a very old-fashioned decorating friend normally seen on pub ceilings. Its rich, undulating patterns look surprisingly modern on a clean-lined piece of furniture like this – particularly when gold leafed.

Leaving camp behind

Although there's plenty of opulence here, it's really only the eye-catching headboard that undulates with historical largesse. Everything else is kept elegant with a highly contemporary sense of sleek, clean-lined chic.

On reflection

Like Alice's door through to Lookingglassford-shire the large, ornately-framed mirror propped in the corner (below) bounces light around the room, helping to open the space out.

Golden oldie

This fabulous floor cushion sums up what is for me a real high-octane, high-impact scheme. It's the kinky combination of gilt leather and slouched comfort that never fails to raise a wry smile. Yes, it's all a bit unapologetically nightclubby, but at least it's the VIP area.

◆ *Painting a wall 148* ◆ *Applying wallpaper 168-9* ◆ *Laying laminate flooring 202* ◆ *Gold leafing 227* ◆

The wonder of one

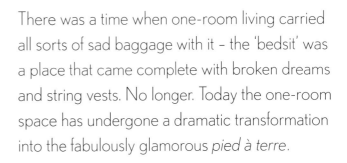

There was a time when one-room living carried all sorts of sad baggage with it – the 'bedsit' was a place that came complete with broken dreams and string vests. No longer. Today the one-room space has undergone a dramatic transformation into the fabulously glamorous *pied à terre*.

Strictly speaking, this wonderful warehouse conversion is five stories away from the *terre* so I suppose it is actually a *pied à ciel*. Whatever you call it, there's a lot of chunky architectural detail in this apartment that has survived the gentrification process from warehouse to swanky flat. All that hewn block work and oaken beamage comes with a strong flavour, so I settled on a mouth-watering colour scheme that can live happily alongside the industrial architectural leftovers. Yellow is never an easy colour in the northern climate. With grey skies and greenish light reflected from all that lush countryside, it can end up terribly acidic. Here, carefully applied blocks of colour bring a sunshine-y warmth to the grey architectural details, while yellow's dominant personality is contained and tamed by its white surroundings. The layout of the apartment, defined by the original architecture, is long and narrow with more than a hint of the corridor to it. So big, brash, bold blocks of colour act to designate zones and create a sense of arrival. All the tricks of the trade have been used here to make sure that light is maximised – furniture has been lifted off the floor on shiny legs and light-reflecting surfaces abound, while a sunlight-intensifying, darkly glossy wooden floor makes the space feel open, light and bright.

Here comes the sun

In this room, light is of paramount importance. Even the display shelves have been conceived so that they won't block precious light or cast gloomy shadows. And the rich, yellow colour block creates an eye-catching feature for the middle of the wall. Sprinkled yellowy greens and the odd lime accent calms the potentially tricky yellow down, making it feel more natural and less acidic.

Despite being up in the sky, this apartment does suffer from being overlooked by others. As light is at such a premium in this space I designed this laser-cut screen as a portable, contemporary take on the net curtain. The screen blocks the specific problem area, leaving the rest of the window to flood light into the room.

Sun-kissed sunflowers

These self-adhesive wall stickers of rather William Morris inspired sunflowers gave me an excellent opportunity to bring a bit of pattern and interest to the walls without cluttering them up. Having just the odd motif as here means the eye-catching texture of the exposed block wall isn't being fussed or over-complicated by an adjacent pattern.

On the level

As a way of grappling with the long, narrow layout, the kitchen sits on a raised level of slate tiles. This change in height and difference in materials peps up what might otherwise be a rather samey-feeling space. It also provides concealment for services like gas, water and electricity through to the long, narrow working unit and creates a boundary between kitchen and corridor.

Shiny happy people

The modern furniture in glossy plastic and light-reflecting lacquer gives this scheme what the previous generation would refer to as Space Age chic...rather funny really. But this classic retro-inspired look in the context of the all-white integrated kitchen does have a kind of NASA-y charm along with an inbuilt ability to bounce back those rays.

◆ Painting a wall 149 ◆ Installing a bracket shelf 198 ◆ Laying laminate flooring 202 ◆

*A*ll natural ingredients

Here a basement kitchen proves that beige needn't be boring if texture is used to bring a bit of touchy-feely sensuality to a scheme.

When you think about it, Nature's never dull. Everywhere you look, light and shadow bring life to every surface. Naturally rough, smooth, shiny or matt surfaces create a constantly scintillating palette of contrasts. In this kitchen, somewhat cursed by an urban basement view, I used Mother Nature as a muse and sought out eye-pleasing pieces which possess an often wry relationship with natural objects. Like those highly amusing root vegetables that can often take on the accidental form of something rude, a similar enjoyment of simulacra works brilliantly here. Vases that look like blades of grass, bowls that look like dock leaves and a candlestick that could fool a cactus spotter all help to bring a healthy outdoor breeze into a downstairs world that could have otherwise felt like a sunless, subterranean burrow. A neutral earthy colour scheme has been used here to continue the natural theme. Decorating like this is notoriously difficult. Naturals, neutrals, beiges, taupes or 'greiges' (grey-ish beiges) all have their own colour top note – what looks like a completely colourless linen can be quite unapologetically green if put next to a beige that errs towards pink, for example. Thankfully here the neutrals all have a close kinship with yellow and green, which ensures that they all get on well together.

3

*B*eware beige blindness

Natural or neutral tones respect tough love decorating, so don't fear strong emphatic contrasts. The black/brown tiling behind the Aga and the dark, shiny slate used for the work surfaces both help to nudge the paler shades into the far distance. They've been used to deliberately command attention and take the eye to the focal point created by the range. Likewise an astroturf-esque rug breaks up the wood laminate floor and brings some colour (and a little of the outdoors) into the room. The use of contrast in this space is essential; without it, the room would slackly unravel into an amorphous beige blob.

Cutting corners

Fitting fitted kitchens requires a lot of thought. While putting the cooker or range into the room's original chimney breast has many advantages, these chimney breasts are rarely deep enough to take modern appliances. For a nice, neat and consistent line, I had the face of the chimney breast brought forward to create a generous surround. This frames the range as well as giving a neat, upright to finish the storage units on either side.

Sitting pretty

I love kitchens that feel like sitting rooms, and as we now spend so much time in them why shouldn't we furnish our kitchens with something a little more comfortable to sit on than simple kitchen chairs? Here a generously upholstered banquette (below) brings a note of soft comfort to the space. As the banquette is built around a radiator with a grill on top, its real gift is most apparent in winter, when it becomes a a fabulously heated seat.

Fridge drawers

In unashamedly naked aluminium, fridge doors (below left) have been conceived to fit alongside the kitchen units. This does away with the need for a tall, visually obstructive fridge and allows for uninterrupted runs of slate work surface that provide the neat, sleek, tailored look that fits this kitchen's scheme.

Bath night at the opera

This is for anyone who feels that come bath time they want to be a diva with a loofah, a Carmen in a shower cap or a Brunhilde in her birthday suit with nothing but a lot of bubbles to cover up her aria.

Think of the great icons of femininity and the odds are that you'll think of them in the bath (well, at least I always find I do). Cleopatra, Messalina, Lucrezia Borgia, Lady Hamilton, Marilyn Monroe – they all conjure up sensual images of indulgent bath times. From the quivering slicks of twinkling bubbles to the rare, exotic unguents in voluptuous-looking vessels, the truly glamorous know that nothing suits them better than a tub and nothing else. Here I've quite shamelessly exploited the theatrical potential to be wrung from a freestanding red lacquered bath in an all-black bathroom. Patterns undulate in feminine whiplashes, while straight lines are kept to a well-edited minimum so that the entire environment works hard to celebrate the decorative potential of womanly curves. This is an unapologetic fantasy room – a highly contrived cocoon in which to escape the grey, grim reality of twenty-first-century living. And why not? The very act of bathing is to immerse oneself into a warm, scented comfort zone as an antidote, an escape, a recharge. The difference here is that the the bathroom *looks* as sensually indulgent as bath time always feels.

4

Beauty from within

Unfortunately the cluttered-up reality of bathing is a thousand and one ugly bottles containing everything from nit shampoo to contact lens solution. In this bathroom, panels pop open to reveal the purple interiors of generous cupboards (below right) which can be called upon to discreetly but conveniently contain such unattractive necessities.

(Shower) curtain call

Since the bathroom opens straight from the next-door dressing room, the heavy-panelled architecture that visually divides the two immediately feels like the proscenium arch of a theatre. The fact that the bathroom steps up causes people to assume I've created a stage to match. In fact the raised floor level is purely practical, accommodating the plumbing and pipe work, as well as the very necessary support beams put in to stop the heavy bath (made heavier when full of water) from crashing through to the floor below.

Down the line

Just about the only straight lines in this bathroom decorate the black lacquer panelling (far right). Providing a light-reflecting touch of opulence, these were actually very easily created with the help of a gold marker pen and ruler. Perhaps more than anything else it's these luxurious twinkles of gold that make this bathroom look like a box at the opera.

◆ *Painting woodwork 150* ◆ *Hanging a mirror 196* ◆ *'Gold leaf' lining 230* ◆ *Covering a lampshade with wallpaper 234* ◆

Reflected glory

An alcove lined with black mirror contains a bulbous modern basin to my design and an ultra-contemporary tap. I had the mirror drilled so that I could then hang an antique framed Venetian mirror on top for a clearer reflection. Since the bathroom is open to the rest of the master suite, both the WC and the basin have tucked away to the sides of the room. This ensures they remain out of sight in the wings, leaving the red-lacquer diva bath very much centre stage.

Beating the cistern

The modern lavatory I designed for this bathroom features a cistern that has been concealed behind a panel. By bringing the wall forward far enough to conceal this I was also able to create yet more storage behind it in the shape of another purple lacquered cupboard. I loved the idea of including a sudden and unapologetic splurge of modernity like this within such a theatrical scheme.

ℒiving in the closet

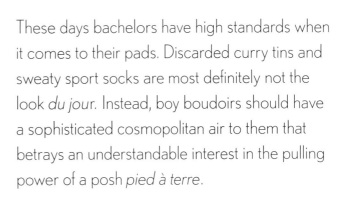

These days bachelors have high standards when it comes to their pads. Discarded curry tins and sweaty sport socks are most definitely not the look *du jour*. Instead, boy boudoirs should have a sophisticated cosmopolitan air to them that betrays an understandable interest in the pulling power of a posh *pied à terre*.

This highly convenient apartment occupies a relatively small ground plan. So, like a Swiss Army penknife, rooms fold away when not in use. The sleeping area is easily separated from the living and cooking quarters by giant, fuchsia-lacquered folding screens. For this scheme I wanted to bring a restrained sprinkling of pattern and interest to the walls without cluttering anything up. So I took inspiration from sportswear and painted what I suppose could only be described as 'go faster' stripes over the bed. Naturally these have resulted in more than a few wry comments, but aesthetically they help to unify a space that could have felt disjointed, with a minimum of fuss and bother. Casually casting around for something to bring interest, I hit upon the idea of heraldry. The clubby connotations of coats of arms also provide considerable design potential in this simple stripped-back scheme. The shields on the walls were created with stencils and pick up the brown, silver and red colour scheme as well as forging a preppy relationship with the gorgeous heirloom antique drums casually used as tables. This is a room where there's just about the right amount going on. It's not actually minimal but neither is it a fruit salad buffet of high maintenance clutter. The perfect compromise for today's metropolitan, urbane neo-dandy.

5

Seeing stripes

Using low-tack masking tape, a straight edge and coloured emulsion paint, these stripes are a more or less instantaneous way of bringing emphasis to a room. The use of thick bands and thinner lines imparts a decidedly retro 80's feel that sits well in this loft-esque context. On-the-diagonal stripes like these create maximum impact with minimum means, leaving enough bare wall around them to keep the feel open and spacey.

Human shield

The coffee table top with its magnificent coat of arms is in fact a large digi-print under glass. Heraldry has a graphic richness that balances detail with crisp, clean lines. It is, I reckon, the ultimate in boy badges. The linen cushions on the sofas were also very simply made using graphic, heraldry-inspired blocks of fabric appliquéd onto shop-bought cushion covers.

History lesson

In uncompromisingly modern spaces like this I always like to insert an object or two that doesn't rhyme with contemporary taste and that has a romance or history that takes it far beyond the here and now. I loved these wonderful drums on sight and knew they'd be a perfect point of interest in this urban yet urbane scheme. There aren't many opportunities for embellishment and pattern in the boyzone, so plundering military history like this is an effective way of injecting a bit of guy glamour into this room.

◆ Painting stripes 159 ◆ Stencilling 164 ◆ Making your own wallpaper with laser transfers 176 ◆ Laying laminate flooring 202 ◆

Contemporary cocoon

Time was the countryside was seen as a backwater. Taste, it was thought, ended at the first sighting of open space while style, if it existed at all in the country, was of the old money variety - tweedy, shabby, but never chic.

But all that's changed. There now exists a new breed of rural retreaters who expect their country environment to come with as much style as a city centre hip hotel. Here amongst the rural idyl a tumbledown old stone building has been swishly reincarnated as an uber-chic chill-out zone. The textures and particular architectural details of the agricultural vernacular typical of the area are left to speak for themselves. But by using the soft, cool, tailored furniture you'd typically expect to see in a modern metropolitan loft, the mellow history of the stone walls and the oak beams becomes heightened by contrast. There's an erogenous commitment to ensuring that this place can be enjoyed as a comfort zone. Sofas as big as beds frame an enormous contemporary fireplace set into the old stone walls, while the lighting is kept low key and sexily amber coloured to ensure the mood remains lusciously laid back. The only note of energy in this space are the cavorting sculptures that have been dotted around to cast deliberately abstract, excitingly curvaceous shadows in the warm, glowing half light.

6

Country house decorating gets hip

It's a real country house classic – a pair of comfortable sofas placed at right angles to a generous fire. Snuggled as close as possible to the warmth of the flames, it's the perfect arrangement for conversation, relaxation or post-Sunday-lunch coma. The breezy width of circulation space behind each sofa ensures that the attention is focused firmly into the centre of the room.

Light-fingered lighting

Getting the lighting right makes a room. Here the rich, orangey glow of the fire has inspired lighting choices that work hard not to shatter the seductive atmosphere. Amber glass globes resonate a rich warm light whilst up lighters installed in the floor are used to caress the textures of the walls. There's nothing harsh, nothing overhead, nothing to break the spell. To be honest, locating a lost contact lens takes an age in this glamorous gloom but that's always going to be a problem in chill-out zones such as this.

◆ *Cleaning a surface for painting 146* ◆ *Painting a wall 149* ◆ *Flaming and staining floorboards 206* ◆

Refined dining

At the other end of the room a light well creates a bright, elegant dining area to contrast with the snug, fire-lit atmosphere it leads onto. By using this kind of twentieth-century thoroughbred furniture the dining area feels like a metropolitan oasis of sleek chic, which only serves to make the mothering warmth of the fire feel that much more compelling.

Techno-deco

Stadium concert-quality surround sound and movie premiere level home cinema have been tactfully integrated in this high-tech, yet old-world space. A lattice of beams on the ceiling conceal wiring and speakers, whilst the great techno engine room that runs the show is discreetly veiled by a hand-forged contemporary screen. On a window sill a retro radio remains permanently tuned to The Archers. It's an oddly piquant statement of retro over techno: the radio we love to see, all those matt black woofers and graphic equalisers we'd actually rather hide.

Busy bathroom

This family bathroom has to change from being a busy, efficient machine for scrubbing and brushing in the morning into a sensual, watery retreat for a hardworking mum at bath time.

Whilst being light, bright and convenient is all any of us need from a bathroom during the morning scramble when the emphasis is on getting ready and getting out, we'd all prefer something more inviting for an evening bath-time treat. Part of the problem is all that white. The bath, the basin, the loo, the tiles – if you're not careful a typical bathroom can give you snow blindness. Here I've used a sleek, elegant grey that reflects daylight when needed but then also looks wonderfully sophisticated in the evening. It doesn't compromise the clean, modern feel of the space, but it does knock the edge off the overlit operating theatre atmosphere that white bathrooms suffer from at night. It's also the perfect foil for the citrus-rich orange shades I wanted to include to invigorate the family's eyes in the morning. Since part of my brief was to persuade the children to be a little tidier, I commissioned a charming hand-drawn mural that shows them how to do it, illustrating clutter neatly put away on shelves. Throughout the mural there are loads of family references and in-jokes to keep a smile on everyone's face, while all the family are encouraged to help themselves to the pot of white marker pens and add to the artwork for a really personal touch. The result is a family-centric bathroom space that is flexible enough to accommodate four very different personalities.

7

Bath-time banter

To really get mum in the mood for a fabulously indulgent evening bath-time soak, there's a sketched bottle of wine at the ready and a prettily drawn decorative table on which to put a bath-time chocolate bar. It's in-jokes and witty references like these that can make a scheme like this such fun for the whole family. Remember, if at any time the joke falls flat, you can always paint the offending item out.

Oodles of doodles

The inevitable storage solutions we all take for granted in bathrooms have here been incorporated into the giant doodle. Cabinets and shelves exist as drawn as well as real elements. Drawing the clutter in a room is an amusing way of encouraging the younger bathroom inhabitants to keep the real, less attractive clutter under control, providing a specific example of how and where things such as towels and toothbrushes should be stored.

In the frame

A jolly over-grand frame brings a note of graphic glamour to what is otherwise a very ordinary piece of high street mirror. Since the markers are always on hand and since they can be so very easily painted over, there's nothing to stop shopping lists, homework diaries, timetables or *aide-mémoire* notes from finding their way onto the walls.

Fun to store

Buckets sprayed in shiny orange enamel have been painted with the children's names to encourage them to look after and take responsibility for their own bath time clutter. This is a great way of sorting out differences of opinion as to ownership (shall we say) and helps to get them used to putting things away.

◆ Painting a wall 149 ◆ Tiling 180 ◆ Hanging a mirror 196 ◆ Laying laminate flooring 202 ◆ Installing a roller blind 222 ◆

Like a lot of spaces that have been converted into apartments from old warehouses, this one's beaming from eave to eave. However, the danger of this vogue for letting it all hang out when it comes to beams, brackets and girders is that it can often lead to rooms that fall short of cosy.

When I first saw this room it was a case of contrast taking a step too close to the edge of edgy – a complex cat's cradle of dark beams set against Hollywood-smile white plaster. To jump the gap between beam and wall (and to bring the sloped ceiling in for a warming goodnight cuddle), I painted over the brilliant white with a rich shade of Beaujolais Nouveau. My design inspiration for this room was the oaky barrel flavour of the rich timber used to panel in the bedhead. Oh, and the fact that this former wine warehouse still seemed to ooze delicious hints of rich, red alcohol. Perhaps I was imagining it. Perhaps it was just thirst, but the final scheme has a scrumptiously strong taste to it with colours that have been chosen to hold eye, nose and throat in flavourful awe. It's a good illustration of how shades from the same chromatic vineyard can be used to bring rich depths and fruity top notes to a scheme. Notice the blueberry-purple cushion amongst all those rich sweet shades of Rioja, a tart accent that surprises and uplifts the room. Finally, glowering in the shadows, a collection of copper objects, despite their more traditional 'kitchen-y' associations, work extremely well in this masculine bedroom.

8

A bon viveur bedroom

Handy headboard

The rich timber boxing used as a headboard disguises all sorts of structural bits and bobs I won't begin to bore you with. Suffice to say that, thanks to the attic-like geometry of the slanting roof, the headboard is able to accommodate pocket shelves built into either end (right) which are useful for storing alarm clocks, bedtime books and glasses of night cap. Meanwhile, the top of the headboard makes for a wonderful place to create an ever-changing still-life display. A dramatis personae of objects awaiting a walk-on part include a variety of copper vessels, a wonderful arts and crafts bowl and a Welsh dragon pastry cutter, while a collection of framed drawings from the late arts and crafts era create the backdrop against which the still-lifers perform.

◆ *Painting a wall 149* ◆ *Making your own wallpaper with laser transfers 176* ◆ *Hanging a picture 196* ◆

Best cellar

Wine labels are designed to look thirst-makingly delicious and during *la belle époque* (the end of the nineteenth century to its friends) they flourished. In order to bring a little of that historical glamour to this bedroom, I scanned some of my favourites labels before printing them onto laser tranfer paper to turn them into instant wall transfers. When placing these on the walls, I went for balance rather than symmetry, ensuring that the density of motifs wasn't any greater in one place than another. Notice also the cushion on the bed. Here a personalised *toile du juoy* pattern has been created by printing a motif onto laser transfer paper. This has then been attached to the dough-coloured glazed chintz of the pillow fabric by ironing on from behind the image.

Rougie bougie

Nestled in the dormer, a pair of Edwardian corner chairs make an elegant settle from which to check out the view of the docks below. There are perhaps those who would question a red light in a dockside window...but not me. The ruby lustre of the lamp base looks just as good when the sun is out and the bulb is unlit as it does when lighting up the room at night.

*R*etro retrod

There are those who find the deliberate revival of the styles of our childhood rather worrying. But why not fill a family comfort zone with references to happier days?

This magnificent kitchen living space expresses the ultimate in contemporary architectural chic. It ticks off an impressive number of the boxes that appear on today's style wish list – lots of light, acres of space and loads of glass – as well as coming complete with some excitingly understated detailing. The tendency for rooms like this to lack soul has been countered here with a bravura attitude to decorating. Wallpaper inspired by the geometric patterns of the late '60s helps to bring the longest wall forward in a friendly, familiar embrace, while vintage accessories, as well as contemporary elements with a retro spin, help to give the room a sophisticated sense of lived-in fashionability. Finally, a relaxed attitude to the cushions and fabrics used on the seating unit helps underline the fact that this room has to be both affable family space *and* high-end design statement. There is a temptation to under-decorate and under-furnish contemporary rooms such as this, ultimately creating a somewhat sterile space that you feel obliged to live up to. By allowing in controlled clutter, this slick scheme succeeds in being high design, but not high maintenance.

9

Why retro's better than vintage

Retro (as in design designed to look old) will always have the edge on vintage, the real stuff from the period. Here this luxurious kitchen in stripy zebrano veneer and stone goes so much further and is so much more convenient that the sort of late 1960's kitchen that inspired it. It's like looking back at the fashion magazines of the past. Sure, I'm often struck by how nice the clothes are, but it's always painfully obvious that what fashion needed most was the invention of conditioner. Fly-away hair? Never.

Pattern on pattern

An extremely relaxed attitude to mixing pattern helps to give this room a marvellously informal feeling. The table runner carries all the colours of the wallpaper but its stylised, natural curves – which take inspiration from the modernist designers of the Art Deco period who influenced the geo-chic patterns of the 60s – couldn't be further from the paper's rectilinear forms.

Glass act

The oak stairs up to the hallway boast a seamless glass balustrade
that gives an uninterrupted sense of space throughout the area.
Glass has been cleverly used here so as not to compromise the
light levels of such a long, narrow room, and creates enclosure
without visually constraining the space.

Let's hear it for the design

People often forget that design can be heard as well as seen. Ultra-
contemporary interiors with lots of hard shiny surfaces create chilly,
uncomfortable acoustics that can be at odds with relaxed family
living. Bundles of cushions, shaggy shag pile rugs, big linen lamp
shades – even canvasses on the wall – all help to absorb sound
and create a space that is more conducive to chatter and children.

What happens when you find yourself sharing your hallway with historic wallpaper? Do you live with it? Live up to it? Or can you somehow make it work?

The temptation here was to either start again and hide all those twittering birds behind something more contemporary, or (worse still) do a Victorian version of 'Pimp my Hall' and make this space into a travesty of 19th-century taste. My solution was to suggest that this young couple shy away from compromise and confront the historicised atmosphere with ultra-contemporary furniture. The result is a space that relies on a strong sense of improbability for its success. The simple geometry of the modern ice white pieces becomes coolly refreshing, its crisp simplicity acting as antidote to the aviary context of the undulating 1870's paper Like a starched white shirt brought up to date by a richly patterned tie, this elegant, highly fashionable scheme revels in the incongruity of space age furniture in a costume drama context.

10

Making an entrance

Invisible switches

Switches, sockets or plugs have a tendency to upstage heavily patterned wallpapers, so an ideal solution is to use elegant switches with acrylic wall plates which let the paper show through. They give necessary technology a tough love lesson in discretion.

$\mathcal{T}$he call of the hall

Never forget that unlike rooms that one sits in one place in, hallways have an audience constantly on the move. They're transitional spaces that don't have one particularly dominant viewpoint or axis. Keep hallway design on the hoof with points of interest to brighten what is an ever-changing interior vista as you move around the space. As you don't spend a lot of time in them, hallways and staircases can profit from a big brushstroke attitude to interior design. Try treating them to schemes where your normal design comfort zone has been expanded or where the colour knob gets turned up a bit – they'll love you for it.

◆ Painting woodwork 150 ◆ Applying wallpaper 168-9 ◆ Hanging a picture 196 ◆ Flaming and staining floorboards 206 ◆

Past and present: a very modern marriage

I've always believed that the past would be extremely surprised to find itself treated with the awed respect we show it today. Back in the 1870's when this wallpaper was created, design legacy was being constantly brought up to date as new styles came into fashion. These days we're either one thing or another – ultra-contemporary or fundamentally traditional. This hall proves that by making room for both in the same space, chic can be elegantly achieved .

Do do a dado

Halls need to be practical. They get a real hammering from people straight from the wet or muddy great outdoors. Dado panelling is macho enough to cope with most things and was invented to provide a practical panelled finish for rough-and-tumble rooms like hallways. My tip for hallway dados is to paint them in heavy-duty emulsion rather than high-maintenance gloss. Any bumps or marks can then be quickly and easily touched up – which with modern paint is as easy as easy maintenance gets.

Well-hung halls

When you are hanging pictures in a hallway, bear in mind that they will be viewed at an ever-changing eye level. As you go up a staircase, hanging a suite or set of pictures in an ascending block increases the sense of height as well as giving you something diverting to look at on the way to bed.

A secret lair with flair

Why is it that the devil gets all the best tunes and villains get all the best pads? Whilst noone remembers what James Bond's place looks like, Dr No, Goldfinger, Blofeld et al have left us with a lasting impression of *grande luxe* interiors found inside some of the most surprising secret lairs.

A former windmill tarted and turreted up by a Victorian landowner as a view-enhancing folly, this part-conversion part-new build is the perfect background for some opulent, villain-inspired decorating. The temptation with a space like this is to try and match the modernity of the architecture to furniture and furnishings that show far too many bolts. So-called modernist design 'classics' (more deserving of the term clichés) would have made this open plan living room irritatingly predictable. Instead French nineteenth-century furniture – with its frivolous gilding and poisonous green damask upholstery – has been used to luxe up this lounge and force the envelope we've marked 'good taste' to be opened and its contents re-examined. This scheme is not, however, as simplistic as old-furniture, new-house. Modern pieces feature heavily but these have been chosen principally for their well-tailored discretion. Like perfectly conceived contemporary display cases in a modern museum of Victorian taste, the sleekly simplistic sofa, ottoman, dining table and chairs in this space all offer the perfect perch for the display of ornate opulence that brings this room alive.

11

Home cinema

This room unabashedly takes its interior inspiration from film, and why not? Some of the most iconic design moments have been entirely motivated by the medium. The golden age of Bond gave the world some astonishing interiors and it was the decadent modernism of the villain's lair that has remained one of my evergreen aesthetic inspirations. With taste as good as their characters were bad, the classic Bond villain surrounded himself with the exquisite, the *recherché* and the obviously recently stolen. It's touches like the gilded, green damask upholstered wooden chair – which, like a time traveller, has somehow found its way into this twenty-first century underground eco-home from a Parisian salon in the 1890's – that capture this feeling and help to make this space so energetically sexy.

◆ *Painting a wall 149* ◆ *Hanging a mirror 196* ◆ *Tiling 180* ◆ *Covering a lampshade with wallpaper 234* ◆

Cabinet of curiosities

Deliberately using things in a room scheme because they're interesting rather than pretty or indeed the height of fashion really floats my boat. For the Georgians, a cabinet full of often quirky, sometimes costly, but always extraordinary objects was their answer to TV – the minerals, fossils and taxidermically preserved marvels had to capture the attention and fill the long nights. This glass-fronted shop cabinet filled with stalactites is a blast from the Georgian past.

Socket and see

Strangely the thing that gives me the most pleasure about the image below isn't the fabulously sexy cast-acrylic standard lamp in the shape of a Baroque candlestick; it's not the elegant Louis *quell-que-chose* console table, it's not even the green damask chair, it's the sockets. In case you hadn't noticed, this is the twenty-first century and we need to be able to accommodate power sockets, telephone connections, CAT cables, SCART points and ISDN lines. Fine as far as I'm concerned, but let's make them part of the design from the outset. Here a guardsman's line-up of electrical possibilities are lined up waiting for the great switch-on.

Table manners

A sleek, contemporary glass dining table comes alive with a decadent Baroque table-scape of gold, gold and, well, more gold. Obviously one's knee-jerk reaction in this space would be to set the table with dignified modernist cutlery in shades of Scandinavian. But there's no word for feast in the dictionary of minimalism, so why not raise the ghost of dinner parties past and give this modernist placement the opulent makeover it deserves?

Ultra violet

In this mid-nineteenth-century town house I was asked to create a scheme that would celebrate the room's impressive proportions, make an elegant background to entertaining and have wow factor by the spade-full.

Rooms like this are made for wallpaper. The Victorian era when this house was built was the great heyday of pattern, and I've always found that just painting walls in rooms this size often leaves them feeling flat and uninhabited. The unusual decision to opt for violet came from out of the ether, yet I knew that to balance such a decadent colour the room would need a sophisticated application of slate grey. This wallpaper is one of my own designs and I'm extremely fond of it. While the scale of the repeat works just as well in high- or low-ceilinged spaces it's the colours – the twinkle of cool gold and gloss black – that make for such an elegant statement. As is often the case with houses of this age, the deep alcoves either side of the chimney breast don't quite match. Papered in with the walls, the chunky shelves help to rebalance this anomaly and provide a stage upon which theatrical groupings of carefully chosen objects can be choreographed. I'm extremely fond of papering shelves or bookcases like this. It's an instant, easy and hugely economical way of finishing MDF or timber shelving that looks great. These days veneering shelves in rich showy woods is extremely expensive, while simply painting them, I think, just doesn't look right. This is the sort of project I relish, where a contemporary sensibility has to be elegantly fused with a room's historical proportions.

12

Balancing act

Symmetry works hard to promote a sense of dependable decorum and pleasure in any room. Here Victorian furniture is given a restrained makeover with purple suede, black velvet and slinky satin. Although the furniture in this room doesn't always exactly match itself either side of a centre line, I've worked hard to give this space a feeling of balance. Thanks to the street-facing windows, this ground floor room can suffer from a lack of privacy when the shutters are opened. Instead of resorting to drab net curtains, a lush window box of lavender helps to partially obscure the view from outside in, while still allowing plenty of light into the room.

◆ *Painting a wall 149* ◆ *Applying wallpaper 168–69* ◆ *Covering a shelf with wallpaper 172* ◆ *Gold leafing 227* ◆ *Faking white gold leaf 227* ◆

By prior arrangement

While symmetry may not always be possible, balance is. Compositions of objects work when the visual weight of one side is balanced on the other. On this cabinet visual equilibrium has been achieved by balancing the large lamp and shade with a collection of photo frames.

Sense of proportion

This room has a heavily ornate cornice typical of its period. To lighten the visual load and to make the room feel even taller, I painted half of it the same shade as the wallpaper. This visually pushes the ceiling up, making it seem further away.

All that glitters

Clusters of reflective, twinkling objects continue the theme of metallic luxury started by the wallpaper. Silver baubles and frames adorn a variety of surfaces while a shamelessly opulent handful of different shades of gold bring life to the marble mantelpiece (left). There are few decorating projects more satisfying than working with gold leaf. Though it obviously doesn't come cheap, it will make a dramatic impact in any room – even when used in small quantities. And if you long for the lustre of all things gold and glittery but don't quite have the budget for the real thing, fear not – it can be effectively (and affordably) faked.

All too often the shower room is a corner stolen from another room...and it looks it. An internal window-free showering capsule has become something of a contemporary necessity. But there's no reason why this space – one of the smallest rooms in the house – shouldn't have the biggest impact.

Like a lot of shower rooms, this space was really just a collection of sanitary ware before I got my hands on it. With no windows, no architectural details and no personality, it made for a perfectly blank canvas onto which I painted an evocative interior inspired by *grande luxe* travel, opulent finishes and Art Deco glamour. Budget forbade expensive marble panels on the walls and the light-reflective marble floor I might have opted for, so instead marbled wallpaper with glistening foil veining was cut into squares and then stuck onto the wall in an alternating chequerboard of eau de nil and ebony – a classically exotic Art Deco colour combination inspired by the waters of the River Nile and the fabulously recherché brown/black of African hardwood. The diagonal lattice theme also makes it onto the vinyl tiled floor. Though the look may be retro, there's a lot of very up-to-date kit in this space. Under-floor heating (which works brilliantly under vinyl tiles) warms the air, whilst an electronically controlled plumbing system provides carefully calculated hot water at the touch of a button – doing away with the visual clutter of taps. The chilly expanse of glass that we're so used to seeing in showers has been turned into an Art Deco screen inspired by one I'd seen on the Orient Express. But rather than budget-busting Lalique, this is a vinyl transfer made from my design by a local signage company.

13

*H*ero of the shower

Trompe l'eau

Visual tricks aplenty have been used to give this tiny shower room character and a greater sense of space. Either side of the door with its digi-print panel of Venice at high water, a pair of highly convenient cupboards hold towels and the electronic nerve centre for the hot water system. A black painted skirting is easily mistaken for additional floor space, whilst the chequerboard papers camouflage and distract the perspective of this full-but-tailored space.

Cool metal

Believe it or not, you can clash taps. While bathroom fittings might all look the same colour, they'll often be slightly different shades of silver. Here shades of nickel and white gold leaf exist happily alongside the chrome highlights of this modern bathroom, knitting everything together. Mini crystal chandeliers hang glamorously over otherwise unremarkable halogen down lights. The faceted droplets cast shards of rainbow across the silvery reflective surfaces of the shower room and heighten the feeling of being in a *grande luxe* cabin, bound for somewhere glamorously foreign.

Push the button

In this bathroom, rather than the typical cat's cradle of pipes and clutter of taps, a push button electronic plumbing system has been installed and programmed with pre-set temperatures and to a preordained duration, ensuring that water isn't wasted and that baths or basins are never left to overflow.

A touch of glass

The turquoise glass handle is the only hint that a cupboard is lurking behind the marble wallpaper. Building storage either side of a centrally placed door creates a small lobby space which accentuates the feeling of space in the rest of the room. When, as here, the cupboards are given an identical treatment to the walls, they become elegantly assumed into the room's architecture.

This room suffered most cruelly from a very common modern malady - dislocated knock through syndrome. Though this small urban house was crying out for a big living space, I knew it would need nanny-ing to make it work.

Anyone who's ever knocked through will tell you that the space you're left with after the wall goes will forever be haunted by the fact that it wasn't actually born a nice big room. For a start, there are usually two chimney breasts. And then there's the left-over stumpy bits of wall support as well as some nasty ceiling scarring caused by that beam you've had to put in to support the floor above. The truth is, left to their own devices and simply painted some timid, pale shade, knock throughs can be ugly, uncomfortable and badly planned. In this space I've fought hard to seduce the eye and distract the brain into seeing the room as a whole. Bold horizontals from one end to another widen the area, while the mismatched chimney breasts appear to be the same size and proportion thanks to panels covered in striped paper – the large television in one balanced by a bronze smoked mirror in the other. The sense of order, balance and symmetry this creates ensures your mind doesn't ask itself awkward questions about the exact dimensions it sees. These eye-catching striped fire surrounds have then been visibly handcuffed together by low shelves that help frame the central section of wall which has been painted a paler shade to show off a large piece of copper wall art. Contrasting colour is used to great effect in this room, with pale stone walls receding whilst solid lamps of chocolatey wood or stripy pattern catch the eye and direct attention to where it should be focused.

ough

14

Using rhythm to right the wrong proportions

There's nothing our poor fevered brains like more than to be soothed by the calming effects of rhythm and symmetry. Our Ancient Greek forbears knew this well, hence those regularly placed columns. In a fractured space like this one, creating symmetry by repeating the same thing once, twice, or three times - whether that be a cushion, chair or picture - will help to make an awkward, oddly proportioned room feel far more balanced.

Skirting the issue

In this room the floor creeps up the wall in lieu of a skirting board. The result of this is that the narrow space immediately feels that much bigger, as those extra few inches of flooring used as skirting end up looking like additional floor space. Simple, but clever.

Eye spy peacock

Peacock is a rich, sumptuous, heavily indulgent colour that can feel horribly cloying and calorific when used excessively. To ground its exotic flavour, I have applied it in combination with a bitter and powdery black coffee brown. Taking inspiration from the plumage of the peacock himself, acid yellow completes the palette, giving it a citrus back-bite which freshens and cleans up the whole scheme.

Using the middle rule

Flagging down the eye and dragging it into the centre of something distracts it from worrying about the edges. With the hanging of objects, installation of two carpet wells in the centre of the laminate flooring (far left) and through the judicious application of contrasting colour, I have used every trick in the decorating book to beguile the eye into believing the space that it's looking at is so very much bigger than it really is.

DAINTY

My goddaughter - an art student, a DJ and part-time volunteer in the local charity shop - wanted to use as little of her allowance as possible to make a space that reflected her interests, her personality and her belief that 'Marie Antoinette rocks'.

It started with Sophia Coppola's film *Marie Antoinette*, with its lavish pastel-hued evocation of French *ancien régime* decadence set to a thumping backing track of Bow Wow Wow, and ends with this bedroom. Apart from the Technicolor-dyed chandelier and the silver gilt plush Louis armchairs (which were birthday presents), everything in this room has been DIYed. Stencils, laser transfers and freehand doodling have all played a part in making the riotous, constantly evolving wallpaper, whilst the curtains (with a huge helping of help from Mum) grew out of studio leftovers I sent over after design collections had been finalised. It's almost as if having being told when a toddler that writing on the walls was out of bounds has inspired her to this ravishing act of aesthetic revenge. This is graffiti at its most glamorous – fusing the raw energy of late 1970's punk rock with the static charm of the late Roccoco. Even the colour scheme – a twisted, saccharine version of the revolutionary tricolour's red, white and blue (here pink, ivory and Wedgewood) – echoes the punk obsession with defacing the Union Jack. Brimming with ideas, all the elements of this space combine to ask one question. Is this teenage bedroom about punking up taste...or tasting up punk?

15

*P*ost-punk princess

A sleeping beauty

Here a traditional wooden bed has been dramatically transformed with a punk-rock Roccoco headboard drawn straight onto the wall. Some studio scraps of wallpaper have been transformed into the upholstery, while the dark, fairytale embellishments are all courtesy of some late-night sessions with a magic marker. As the artist's godfather I would love to disapprove, but actually I was exactly the same at her age (as indeed was her dad).

Snug as a bug in a rug

The pale colourwashed floorboards of this room were far too tasteful for such a high-octane scheme as this. Using a stencil and black spray paint, an instant zebra skin rug (below right) was created to provide some visual impact and break up the wooden expanse.

L.P. – O.A.P

I never thought I'd see the day when the music of my youth hit on trend status again. As a DJ, a finger on the trendy pulse is a prerequisite, but nevertheless it's still a jolt to see one's goddaughter quite so excited by the post-punk vinyl of my own adolescence. Still, these illuminative frames allow classic vintage vinyl to be celebrated as art, whilst also remaining conveniently accessible should the record in question be worth a hearing.

Never mind the Pollocks, it's the Sex Pistols

Of all the projects and makeover transformations in this room I love this chair the most. The seat has been upholstered (courtesy of Mum) to look like an exquisitely iced birthday cake. But it's the paint spattered frame that impresses me the most. There's nothing complicated or contrived about this very simple technique. Spattering dribbles of paint in a series of sugary shades over what is actually a very humble junk shop chair.

Spring greens

This mouth-wateringly fresh kitchen with its interconnecting dining room is as wholesome and refreshing as a lovely herby salad. Less like an island unit, more like a life-raft, everything's close at hand in the centre of this space.

I really don't like kitchens that look and feel as though they are just machines for cooking in. These days kitchens are nearly always the backdrop to the majority of family living, and so I love to make them into welcoming, flexible spaces that everyone can feel at home in. And that goes for the chef too – where at all possible it's so much friendlier not to force whoever is cooking to be bent double over a pan in a dark corner. Here the cooking apparatus – the hob and two ovens – stand solid and proud right in the centre of the room. Typical space-hogging kitchen wall units have instead been replaced with an acreage of zesty wallpaper (which is repeated on the lampshades of the ironwork chandelier that masks the modern extractor unit), whilst any storage shortfall has been made up by cupboards either side of the fireplace and a whole wall of open shelves between the two spaces. It's a soft, romantic scheme that flirts with a few retro references like the poptastic glossy wall unit doors and the hippy-chick scaled wallpaper repeat, while the gnarly fossil-specked stone of the unit kickboard and flagstones provides the perfect practical counterbalance to the lacy, delicate glamour of the wallpaper and the lacquered modernity of the units. Possessing a lovely sense of the old and the new treating each other with mutual respect, this kitchen is an easy-going place which doesn't require control-freak tidyness or terminal house doctoring to keep it looking great.

$\mathcal{A}$ space of two halves

Rather than even attempt to knock out a grade II listed wall, I have instead created a very generous panelled opening to connect the kitchen with the dining room. On the kitchen side, painted shelves play host to china and glass that get arranged and rearranged in pleasing still lives whenever the dishwasher is emptied. In the easy-going dining room, cookery and gardening books and plenty of pictures give the room a constantly lived-in informality, while spring-fresh wallpaper and judiciously placed mirrors help to bounce light around both spaces.

Why green is great

Green is a real light bouncer –
particularly when it's stuffed full of zingy
yellow as it is here. With white it's
always fresh and chirpy, but notice how
little red I've let into the colour scheme.
Using a similarly toned ozone blue
instead as the main accent colour helps
to prevent the scheme from
degenerating into a rather obvious
essay in shades of traffic light.

Creating symmetry

With the panelled opening (left)
creating an elegant frame, both kitchen
and dining room feel entirely
symmetrical. In reality the opening isn't
anything like as central as it has been
made to look, but has been balanced
and made to look symmetrical by the
shelves and objects that surround it.
This gives the space a rewarding sense
of clean-cut architecture which provides
a satisfying contrast with the frilly
pattern of the wallpaper.

Fabulous finishes

There are some great textures for the
eye to linger over in this relaxed space.
Notice the soft, fudgey stone floor, the
icing sugar patterned wallpaper and the
gorgeous cracklure on the woodwork.
But my favourite finishing touch is the
least expensive, the unit doors. These
have been made from MDF and have
been cut-to-size before being marched
off to the local car sprayer, who gave
them several coats of tough-as-nails,
ultra-shiny cellulose car paint.

Surf shack sophisticate

This seaside family holiday home sits up on the cliffs with a view down to a sea swarming with sun-kissed surfers. As an outpost for beachtime expeditions, this space needed to be homely but uncluttered, chic but low maintenance and to feel as inside/outside, or should that be outside/inside, as possible.

The starting point for this room was the carpet tiles. Yes, that fabulously contemporary art area rug is in fact made up of good old-fashioned, high-impact, low-maintenance, throw-anything-at-them carpet tiles. This means, of course, that were some of that post-surf cocoa to spill and slay a tile there's a box full of willing replacements in the cupboard. But those grey pebbles couldn't be allowed to turn this happy holiday atmosphere drab, hence the gloom-busting pink linen and handful of fuchsia accessories on hand to lighten the mood. Many of the elements of this room have been conceived to be as at home inside as they are on the suntrap sundeck through the large sliding glass doors. All-weather floor cushions in both spaces as well as planters designed to look as much like indoor furniture as possible help soften the transition between outside and inside. Meanwhile the curvaceous whiplashes of collected driftwood boughs make an excellent, almost Art-Nouveau base for a slick, glass coffee table. Part shelter from the elements, part extension of the outdoors, this beach hut is a very happy place indeed.

17

Feeling finely balanced

The exterior of this very contemporary building works within its wonderful landscape as it makes modern shapes using natural ingredients like wood and slate. Inside, slick, sleek elements are softened by the decorative lines and tactile curves of organic pieces such as the driftwood coffee table and the wooden uplighter. Meanwhile, both modern and organic elements are brought together and invigorated by a nice big dollop of raspberry sorbet.

Fringe benefits

Although the views rock, and indeed there is a lot of rock to be viewed, these big picture windows (right) could also offer temptation to prying eyes. To counter this, and to take the edge of that classic gold fish bowl feel that comes with living in a glass house, I found these perfect window-length fringes. Light and airy, they move in the breeze when the doors are open but fall far short of the horrible claustrophobia that is all too often the result of hanging net curtains.

Gnome front

I really wanted to add an element or two to this scheme that would continue the slightly surreal humour of the giant scale pebbles on the carpet tiles. As the budget was tight I was forbidden from finding costly or high-maintenance knick-knacks, so I marched to the nearest garden centre and bought a veritable boy band of gnomes. Nothing fancy – just the cheapest they had. A quick spray with white car spray paint was all it then took to transform them into *the* talking point for anyone coming to tea.

Bench press

Hewn from excitingly wiggly lumps of timber, this sturdy dining table was sourced locally. Since the area often hosts boisterous groups of teenage surfers of indeterminate number, I did away with chairs and decided on good old-fashioned long benches inside. This means that far more people can be squeezed around the table as well as keeping the dining area feeling uncluttered and open.

◆ *Painting a wall 149* ◆ *Laying laminate flooring 202* ◆ *Laying carpet tiles 204* ◆

I was asked to design this modestly modern marina-side property for a couple who really wanted to squeeze the most out of retirement. Their one request was to make the design as tactile as possible. Getting a room right isn't always just a visual art, there's something wonderful about creating a scheme that seduces other senses as well. When faced with a particularly modern room, focusing on it's touchy-feely potential is a wonderful way of welcoming in well-behaved pattern and detail.

With loads of light bouncing in from the water just beyond the deck, I could really indulge this scheme with some wonderfully tacticle details. To start – and as our couple had mentioned that, since retiring, they had both pretty much given up wearing shoes indoors – I decided to install a leather floor which, thanks to underfloor heating, would not only feel delightfuly soft underfoot but would also be fabulously warm in the winter. The beautiful cedar tan leather floor tiles I found are a real treat for the feet that will also end up softening further over time. Becoming involved in a new-build like this at an early stage means that particular architectural elements can be seamlessly integrated into your design scheme. On one wall, a contemporary fireplace as well as a concealed flat screen television (hidden behind a painting and unveiled at the press of a button) were specified as part of the build, which meant both the main focuses of the room could be accommodated within the same visual axis. Moving from a large, traditional family house meant finding new, more modern ways to display a lifetime's collection of bits and bobs gleaned from extensive travels all over the world. It was an exciting opportunity to revisit a large collection of memory-imbued mementos with a fresh eye.

$\mathscr{S}$ilver surfer's surface

18

Blue horizon

To draw attention to this high, airy and light-filled space, I chose a nice, warm blue. There's a lot of yellow in this particular shade, which stops the walls looking icy when skies are grey. Meanwhile an extensive palette of traditional tweeds used for cushions and curtains warms the room up further and provides a rough contrast to the shine of the leather floor.

Balancing act

I chose to hang the highlights of a lifetime's art collection as a portfolio grouping, trying to avoid symmetry but achieve a sense of balance. This is a wonderful way of making old art feel contemporary and is best done by trying out various groupings on the floor in front of the wall first. If you want to try the same thing, remember to set yourself a middle line before you begin and then work from left to right from the middle.

Plinth of tides

On upturned chunky glass vases a collection of bouncy bronze hares is given prominence and shown off to full advantage. Grouping bits and bobs like this at a variety of different heights is a wonderful way of giving smaller objects more emphasis.

The long and the short of it

The tall narrow windows either side of the chimney breast lacked prominence, so I papered the surrounding wall in a heavily textured dark brown grass cloth paper. This not only helps to emphasise these delicate windows, but also brings a further tactile natural note to this very urbane scheme, while hinting at exotic, Far Eastern locations.

◆ Painting a wall 149 ◆ Applying wallpaper 168-9 ◆ Hanging a picture 196 ◆

*M*rs de Winter wonde

Anyone who has seen Alfred Hitchcock's film version of Daphne du Maurier's novel *Rebecca* couldn't help but be transfixed by the spectacular sets. Mandalay, the ominously beautiful house of the late Mrs Rebecca de Winter was the main inspiration for this masterful master bedroom.

Though this large bedroom, originally formed from three smaller rooms, may be set in a stone-built 17th-century manor house, the look is very much luxurious Film Noir. Eye-catching elements such as the simple black chiffon bed drapes and the black carpet plinth that gives the bed such regal presence inject the space with lots of elegant drama, while the room's intricate layers of entrancing patterns have a foliate femininity that – thanks to the rigorous colour scheme of liquorice black, cool oyster, gold and ruby –stops well short of blousy. Curtains in dull gold satin hint at the haute couture styles of the late 1930's and the wallpaper print along with the embroidered bed cushions show a pre-war sensibility, when oriental-inspired floral patterns were the epitome of chic. Inspired directly by the film, 18th-century cabinets flank the bed whilst, hovering above the simplistic black suede-covered headboard, an ornately framed oriental silk painting of the Goddess of the Moon evokes the elegant femininity of the Art Deco period's predilection for the exotic. This room is a highly charged homage to the sort of powerful feminine glamour British literature, and indeed British cinema, celebrated so elegantly in the 1930's.

19

Closet case

Deep, voraciously hungry wardrobes (below) are discreetly underplayed, allowing the floral wallpaper to take centre stage. Touch latches mean obvious handles aren't needed, whilst papering the doors in the same way as the walls before hanging pictures on them means they become invisible. It's a perfect example of the art of 'glamouflage'.

*D*ressing up rooms

When I can't remove a wall but want to open a space up, one of my most reliable tricks is to create an elegantly panelled, generously proportioned door case. Here the adjacent dressing room – with its black lacquer furniture and mirrored cabinets, which hint forcefully that this is the lair of a Glamazon – is theatrically framed. The two areas remain distinct, but feel airy and open thanks to the subtly reflective, pale gold printed paper that pulls them both together.

◆ *Applying wallpaper 168-9* ◆ *Hanging a picture 196* ◆ *Covering a lampshade with wallpaper 234* ◆

Blurring the edges

Thanks to the black carpet border and the matt black skirting board it's almost impossible for the eye to work out where the floor ends and the wall begins. The carpet itself undulates with eye-catching whiplash curves, also ensuring that the attention goes straight to the centre of the space and away from its camouflaged edges.

Ace of shades

Within this refined bedroom, lighting and technology are kept elegant and chic. A pair of modern chandeliers (opposite above) hangs poised over each night table, keeping clutter to a minimum and creating focused beams of light in just the right place for bedtime reading. Taking a little inspiration from a boutique hotel trick, a flat screen television and mini bar share a discrete Edwardian book cabinet at the end of the bed, perfectly positioned for night-time viewing.

From lowly to lovely

This very ordinary suburban 20th-century sitting room has profited immeasurably from the marvellous magic wand of makeover and goes to prove that even the instantly recognisable, spitefully featureless architecture of the last century can be elegantly overcome.

Dark, almost tunnel-like, before I begun work on this very beige box the only thing of note was the interesting architectural salvaged fire surround. It immediately struck me that this space needed more windows, but as the budget for the project was microscopic I forgot about expensive building work and instead installed three mirrors with arched tops that were cut for me by a local glazier. Finally, using self-adhesive lead strips I was able to turn these mirrors into glamorous, orangery-style 'windows' that double the sense of space as well as reflecting lashings of light back into the room from the real windows opposite. Spaces like this lack rhythm, so I used one of my favourite techniques – trompe l'oeil – to carve the wall surfaces up into elegant panels with a three-dimensional appearance. The colour scheme of pale stone, washed golds, corn, hay and beige sprang from a venerable pair of good-quality vintage curtains that I came across in a local curtain exchange (a valuable decorating resource where, aside from any green points that are to be earned from the actual recycling, economically speaking you'll find curtains for a fraction of the new price). The final finishing touch for this room was a veritable greenhouse of exotic plants. In fact, they're very convincing fakes but do a fabulous job of bringing this garden room alive and dissolving the boundary between inside and outside.

20

Reflected glory

To prevent the distraction of catching your own eye in the large architectural mirrors, I have used various garden-themed objects to deliberately obscure the bits where your reflection is most likely to appear. It means all the space-enhancing benefits of the mirror are there to be enjoyed, without the perpetual distraction of narcissism. And narcissism can be very distracting. Here I've used plants and plinths but pictures or clocks can be hung over a mirror for the same effect.

Chanson d'armoire

Created with high-street floating shelves and trompe l'oeil panels which end in the sort of arched tops you often get in French furniture and rustic chateau panelling, this skeletal armoire provides impact without breaking the bank.

Feeling touchy

The high lights, low lights and shadows of a number of natural objects, including this wonderful shell-encrusted mirror, chime elegantly and rather surreally with this room's painted panelling.

Come into the garden, Maude

Using garden acessories like topiaried shrubs and stone planters indoors is a very efficient way of bringing the outdoors indoors and expanding the sense of space in small ground-floor rooms like this one. A garden bench or lead urn on the outside terrace that matches one inside helps to draw the eye and interest out beyond the confines of the room itself.

Net loft chic

A contemporary approach to decorating the kitchen/dining space of this 18th-century Cornish net loft nestling right by the harbour has led to a timeless interior that I absolutely love spending time in.

Sometimes there's no point in sprinkling your kitchen willy-nilly throughout a largish room. In the short length of this L-shaped space I've squeezed a convenient kitchen where all the appliances are within arm's reach. This interior is all about balance; the clean-cut lines of the local slate contrast elegantly with the softly billowing blue-grey painted plaster walls, while the lacquer shine of the dark, varnished floor reflects the random bird's nest of reused ship beams that hold up the ceiling. The view from the window of grey-blue sea, black granite cliffs and opaque expanse of milky-white sky is the inspiration behind this room's simple, graphic colour scheme. The dark timber of the floor carries up onto the cupboard plinths, which means the white-painted MDF kitchen unit doors appear to float, preventing the fitted unit from feeling claustrophobic. And rather than lumpish wall units that always make kitchens look that much smaller, a pair of plank-like open shelves enable the stored china and glassware to become part of the decorative scheme. Painting the knotty, splintery old bits of wood that made up the cealing beams proved to be a nightmare, that is until the decorator and I came up with the idea of mixing a few generous handfuls of Artex powder into the white emulsion, so that it went on in a satisfyingly thick, workable paste.

$\mathcal{L}$earning from minimalism

While by nature I couldn't be less sympathetic to minimalism (it's all a bit too rigid and short on laughs), there is something to be said for clean lines and an eagle eye for clutter. Particularly when these are, as here, balanced by soft, romantic, textures like the blanket curtains that cuddle the windows and the glitzy-glam black Venetian mirror that hangs between them. Oddly, despite the contemporary details, there's something rather Georgian about this space. The well-proportioned long table made especially to fit the room and the satisfyingly simple modern classic chairs add to the air of restrained grace and favour, while the simple chandelier adds a historic touch. It's the sort of scheme I really enjoy - a little bit modern, a little bit Georgian, a little bit country, a little bit rock and roll.

◆ *Painting woodwork 150* ◆ *Installing a floating shelf 199* ◆ *Tongue-and-groove panelling 194* ◆ *Hanging a curtain 223* ◆

Storing in plain sight

For a family-friendly seaside bolthole this may seem impressively orderly, but when space is at a premium it's essential that rooms don't get cluttered up. Storing in plain site like this not only means there's nowhere for extraneous clutter to hide; it also provides an opportunity to play with decorative compositions of different patterns, textures and objects.

Let the air flow

Notice how the furniture throughout this room is very leggy. I wanted to maximise the potential for the light to reflect off the shiny floor; it's amazing what a difference to the sense of space you can make by choosing deliberately thoroughbred, thin furniture with supermodel legs.

Interconnecting

The layout is typically organic and the random progression of spaces is part of the joy of this room, but rigid geometric statements like the table and the diagonal-cut sea grass rug help to anchor what is actually a pretty crazy floor plan.

Stealing views from other rooms

In this open plan space there are some fabulously intriguing glimpsed views from room to room. As a result, I've had a lot of fun taking the kitchen's colour scheme and its palette of textures and playing around with them a bit within the other rooms of the net loft such as this sitting area (below) – like jazz riffs on an original tune.

Shopaholic heaven

And so what is the well-dressed room wearing this season...? Why it's wearing whatever you've just taken off and left casually draped over a chair, of course.

Control freaks with their spic and span lives best look away now, because this room not only revels in the fun of clutter, it also looks totally wrong when neatly tidied up. I've always believed we should all be allowed to surround ourselves with the particular things that bring us pleasure. Here frocks, shoes, handbags and feather boas combine to to create this engaging, eccentric and fabulously fashionable scheme. And why not? Who says that our possessions should be tamed through imprisonment in dark closets? This scheme works because the room is treated to the same sort of glamorous pattern palette and sugary colour choices as the clothes that have escaped from the wardrobe. Quirky ways of showing off these prized possessions, through the use of mannequins and china figurines, means the eye is constantly diverted and amused. The sultry, theatrical reflections from the foil-printed wallpaper give an ever-changing cloudy sky effect as reflections and shadows catch and dance across its shiny surface, creating an open horizon background for the plates of painted birds and boughs, mirrors and picture frames that cover it. This room has an exuberant 'happy hour' atmosphere – part teatime treat, part vintage cocktail vamp – that oozes amused, and amusing, femininity.

22

Squeezing in storage

The neat attitude to storage within this space is very much inspired by the mingling of convenience typical of French dressing rooms. A pair of reasonably sized built-in cupboards – one to hang posh frocks, the other containing a discreet basin (literally a faucet in the closet) – flank the bed in classically inspired symmetry. Stolen alcoves provide necessary space for lamps and bed-time chick lit whilst a moulded architrave frames the bed to give princess-y prominence in the room.

Shopping around for style

An eclectic mix of furniture styles – from romantic antique to clean-cut contemporary – keeps pace with the fact that the occupant's wardrobes mingles plush, post-party frocks on the same rail as 21st-century techno tailoring. Fusion is a very overused word these days, but I have to admit I did really enjoy fusing such contrasting design styles here to make one whole new boho scheme.

Yummy dummy

What better to show off a latest purchase than by displaying it on a recycled shop dummy or mannequin? Dressed and redressed like life-sized Barbies, these objects become fusions of fashion and sculpture within the room.

Bravo for bling

The decadent sparkle of a great deal of paste jewellery finishes this scheme off perfectly. Rather than stuffed away in a box, favourite pieces are draped on a menagerie of china figurines for a sexily surreal effect.

◆ *Applying wallpaper 168-9* ◆ *Hanging a picture 196* ◆ *Upholstering a headboard 218* ◆ *Making a pelmet 220* ◆

Well-mannered manor

Personally, I think it's a little pointless to live in a manor house and not indulge yourself with panelling, antlers, big stone fireplaces, concealed passages and all the things that such a space demands. But perhaps that's just me...

While this manor house great room might have oozed history, thanks to several decades of unsympathetic ownership there was surprisingly little here of architectural interest. Apart from the Cotswold stone fire surround, the room itself was a blank (or more accurately beige) canvas. So, where to start? That the room needed bookcase units to house this huge collection of books was a given. In creating these, I took design inspiration from the bigwigs of history, the taste mongers and style gurus of the seventeenth century (the time when this manor house was built) such as Samuel Pepys, who were all for covering bookcases in fabrics or hand-painting in patterns. Papered in the same custom-designed paper as the walls in rich shades of chocolate and orange, the bookshelves were built in wallet-friendly MDF (as the budget precluded polished timber), and the disparate colours and odd sizes of the books they house make for a randomly patterned, ever-changing wallpaper background to the space. Accessory accents in slippery tangerine lacquer – such as the eye-catching faux-lacquered console table made using printed tissue paper and PVA – bring warm hospitality to the chocolate brown throughout this north-facing room. It's the perfect plinth for the laser-cut iron lamp bases and shades showing continuous views of Venice. Finally, for practicality's sake I bordered the pale, sand-coloured carpet with rufty tufty brown, so that constant journeys in muddy country boots wouldn't make their mark.

23

Sitting comfortably

I chose sofas for this room that would be of a comfortable size, but not so gigantic that they would dwarf the space. Covered in cosy silk velvet, they're the perfect perch for conversation. The large coffee table is, in fact, an old wooden door (carved with the date 1672, which places it around the age of this part of the house) simply displayed on an MDF plinth covered in a piece of carpet. The panels aren't hugely convenient for putting down items that need to balance on a flat surface, so I've placed a series of lacquer trays, books and platters to act as safe perches for those coffee cups or water glasses.

Secret history

This room profits enormously from its uninterrupted blocks of displayed books and art, so using guile to cover the tracts of utilities or dull conveniences is one way of preserving the space's bookish character. The large bookcase behind the sofa conceals a spring-hinged panel door – leading to an odd collection of boot and flower rooms – over which real book spines have been stuck. Meanwhile a simple, gate-hinged flap on which I've hung a framed map conceals a large flat screen television.

Slave to the rhythm

I've drawn attention to the pleasing rhythm created by the four tall windows in this room by using elegant tangerine-lined curtains and by placing bronze radiators in the spaces between each. Stone shelves turn the radiators into console tables, whilst bronze mirror panels on which I've hung ornately framed portraits make a knowing nod in the direction of early Georgian decorating, where light was maximised by placing classical 'looking glasses' between windows.

Pearly queen

Pearls have always been a symbol of femininity. From the sea-born goddess Venus worshipped by the Ancient Greeks for her voluptuousness to the courtesans of *fin de siècle* Paris, the pearl radiates luxuriousness, abundance and multifaceted, multicoloured charm.

When you work hard, it's so incredibly important that the 'my space' you long for looks the way you've always dreamt it would. Unfortunately, this frankly featureless bedroom with its corner bed didn't come close to reflecting either the aspirations or dynamic personality of its inhabitant. To help, I prescribed her a contemporary take on the traditional four-poster bed, using dramatically layered curtains at each corner whilst the bed itself was inspired by the particular, fugitive shades of grey, ivory, pink and aubergine that a pearl mysteriously adopts depending on how it's viewed. It's an extremely sophisticated starting point for a very grown-up bedroom, which requires an assembled a palette of silks, matt velvets and embroidered taffetas to work in glamorous layers. Whilst pearl acts as the colour prima ballerina, the corps de ballet has been made up of silver leaf, mirror, black lacquer and chrome to evoke parallels with the starlets' bedrooms of Hollywood's heyday. This scheme owes a debt to a timeless fantasy of femininity; it's difficult to look at what I've done here and not think boudoir.

24

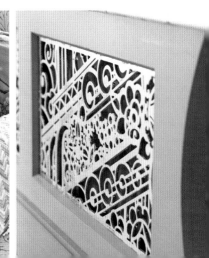

Chinese takeaway

Chinoiserie, a particular term to describe the particularly feminine evocation of oriental style used so exquisitely by the Georgians, here adds another layer of texture. Many of the patterns owe considerable debt to the free-flowing, organic repeats of classic oriental pattern-making. The blossom-studded boughs embroidered on the taffeta pelmets have a very eastern feel whilst the fabulously expensive-looking wall covering is not quite what it seems. A silvery printed paper was hung, then over-stencilled, using off-the-shelf oriental stencils in shades of shell. Doing it yourself means that areas you want to emphasise (such as around pictures) or indeed disguise (such as the room's corners) can receive patterns, whilst the bulk of the wall remains untouched.

◆ *Applying wallpaper 168–9* ◆ *Varnish stencilling 165* ◆ *Hanging a picture 196* ◆ *Making a pelmet 220* ◆

It's a cover up

I couldn't countenance anything as everyday as radiators in this fantasy boudoir, so instead I designed these elaborate cases covered in wallpaper with grills and tops silver-leafed, then shellacked, to look like white gold. Complemented by Roman blinds and pelmets that echo their shape, they become important pieces of furniture in their own right. Meanwhile, the coppery toned, sheer silk curtains serve to hide black-out curtains which are operated by a remote controlled, electric track. Now, when morning comes, the black-out curtains part like the opening frames of a Hollywood premiere.

Mix it up

This room is enlivened with elements drawn from many sources. A Victorian-inspired chaise longue, a distinctly modern dressing table and stool and a Venetian triptych mirror all chat happily together within this space. Although the periods that inspired all these sexy things might be different, they are all linked by a strong, and very palpable sense of femininity.

Summer living had me a

This corner room of an old manor house looks out onto a traditional flower garden. It's the perfect place for summer lunch, so I decided to freeze-frame the moment and decorate this dining room with an 'every day is summer' scheme.

Back in the grand old days, people really did have summer rooms, winter rooms and working rooms – spaces they set aside for a particular time or season. I love this idea, and inspired by the flower borders that sit just beyond the room's windows, I decided to use it here – taking the room outdoors by decorating it with a full-on high-summer pattern. There's something about this archive pattern, when used as here, in juicy abundance, that sits well in a room with this kind of farmhouse-y detailing: anything more refined or floral might run the risk of looking pretentious and busybody-ish. Classic French rural decorating inspired the use of a fabric that matches the wallpaper on the table cloth, curtain edges and lampshades. For those pattern-phobes who'd worry that a matching table cloth is a step too far, bear in mind that a repeat this intense really does need an 'all or nothing' attitude to make it work. The stiffened edging in the room's main-theme pattern creates frames for the windows which are finished off on top by pelmets covered in matching wallpaper. To give the eye an occasional break; white painted furniture, heavy white picture frames and panels below the high-silled windows stop the room from getting too shrill or noisy, while the soft, transparent muslin curtains catch the summer breezes and sun beams, bringing the outside in. These touches, combined with the use of simple rustic sea grass on the floor, place the pattern in context and help create an atmosphere of easy-going, welcoming informality.

blast

(25)

Expanding to suit the guest list

Normally set for six, the round table with the glass-topped cloth gets bumped for bigger do's. I agonised for weeks about getting the right table – something that extended to sit ten was called for, and proved impossible to find. So instead, collapsible catering tables came to the rescue. Here two oblong tables, under an extraordinarily pretty antique lace cloth, sit in anticipation of a lunch party for twelve. Notice, by the way, the duck egg blue cloth (which is actually a simple bed sheet) grinning through the vintage lace.

◆ Applying wallpaper 168-9 ◆ Hanging a picture 196 ◆ Covering a lampshade with wallpaper 234 ◆ Making a pelmet 220 ◆

The enfilade

In France, corridors are treated somewhat with suspicion; I've no idea why. Classic French rooms lead from one to another in a sort of procession which is called an enfilade. This dining room links the front hall to the kitchen hall, so to minimise the potential ruination brought about by muddy Wellingtons and muddier spaniels, a pathway of stone (bordering the seagrass rug that has been laid in the centre of the room) extends from hall to hall.

Indoor/outdoor decoration

A simple formula for keeping this sort of pattern-tastic scheme is to break things up with a little white. With the lampshades, using the same pattern but with a white background helps give the eye a momentary breather.

Avoiding over-coordination

In a scheme like this – with all its fine finishes, twinkling crystal and stacked linen – stealing cheeky bits of the great outdoors by using flowers and butterfly paperweights helps to echo the wallpaper and makes the room feel like a glamorous picnic.

Redressing proportions

Having window sills at hip height shouts cottage loud and clear. This is great if it is cottage you want. I, however, am hooked on long, tall windows with gracious proportions and full-length curtains. Here I have installed moulded panels below the windows to give them greater elegance and give me an excuse for classical, long drapes.

Rose room

When the going gets tough, the tough get burrowing. While big lofty spaces with iconic views of the city centre might be modern, they're rarely snug. Here every trick in the Cosy Book has been used for country effect.

I've always thought that red and white is the colour combination equivalent of comfort food. It takes you back to an ideal of what home should feel like, be it a real or an imagined sensation. Raspberry pureé lacquer paint slathered like jam onto breakfast toast provides the perfect background to a variety of shades of sliced white. Thanks to the romantically rustic tongue-and-groove panelling, this room, like the interior of a red shiny shed, is all about comforting enclosure. It really is (if you pardon the pun) a womb with a view. All the emphasis is on that soft-as-duck-down bed with its heap of cushions, throws and cuddly blankets, perfect for an aspiring sleeping beauty or princess with a real love of retro. There's nothing here that could be thought of as glam, glitzy or indeed terribly grown up, which is what makes it the perfect winter holiday bolthole. It also goes to prove that red is one of the most sociable of colours you can use when decorating your home. No matter how many shades of it you invite to any party, red is a fabulous mixer and will never ever pick a fight with any of its myriad relations. This bedroom quite emphatically flies in the face of conspicuous consumption; it oozes solid positive values like make-do-and-mend and dig-for-victory, while proving once and for all that patchwork is definitely the new rock 'n' roll.

26

Bread and jam

Like windows, the large botanical watercolours in their spacey pale mounts float against the brightly-coloured walls and break up their intensity. The jumble-sale-chic collections of furnishings – including high-street patchwork bedspreads reinvented as curtains and bed drapes – also help bring some fresh air into all that steaming raspberry.

Bewitched by craft

In pattern terms, more really is very, very much more. In this room, shades of white and red are able to unite several dozen different floral patterns - all of which look as though they've got a story to tell about what they were up to before they ended up in this picture-perfect patchwork paradise.

360 degrees on the shade

With so much wonderful pattern in this room, I could never have countenanced using ordinary lampshades. So instead I created my own. Photographs of the local area, interspaced with scanned-in patterns, were printed out onto shiny presentation paper before being stuck over standard, pale-hued lampshades. Now, whenever the light is switched on, the effect is like a patchwork magic lantern show.

◆ *Tongue-and-groove panelling 194* ◆ *Making a no-sew curtain 221* ◆ *Decoupage 228* ◆ *Covering a lampshade with tissue paper 235* ◆

Alice slept here

Playing with scale heightens the fairytale and puts the wonder into Wonderland. Like the botanical pictures, this enormous mirror also helps to open up this room, breaking up the brightly coloured wall and allowing light and space into this red-hued hot house.

Rosey supposey

These large roses were painted on the chest of drawers but they could just as easily have been decoupaged roses that had been scanned, printed out, cut out and stuck onto the chest using PVA adhesive for some custom-made chintz. Notice how painting the chest the same colour as the walls has made this potentially bulky piece of furniture retreat quietly into the background.

If there's one thing young children have been specifically programmed to destroy it's the parental peace of a weekend lie-in. No matter how boring the working week, in the morning there they'll be – perky, beady and after attention.

This bedroom, with its cleverly integrated bathroom, has been conceived to look coolly chic, but to also be perfectly convenient for a bouncy young family. A large flat screen television tuned to cartoons in perpetuity, generous leather-covered toy storage and convenient loo all cater to the boisterous demands of early riser toddlers. Meanwhile Mum and Dad can relax in comfortable, monochrome luxury. All that white might at first glance seem very un-toddler friendly – but all is not quite as it seems. For a start, all the leather in the room is faux, as tough as, well, boots and also very easily cleaned, while that white shag pile carpet is actually made up of white shag pile carpet tiles. So should there be any crayon or blackberry juice damage; the offending imperfect tile can be easily replaced from a box of pristine new ones.

Escaping the parent trap

Having your minimalist cake and eating it

My brief was to reconcile a highly contemporary decorating stance with the practicalities of family living. The all-black tiled bathroom at one end of an all-white room is a wonderfully chic statement that becomes a perfect calming oasis within the hubbub of young family life. This scheme was a matter of parental pride for me. I very much wanted to prove to the young parents of the planet that a designed environment, a space where aesthetics can be integrated along with the nappy bags is possible and reasonably easy to achieve.

Peek a boo

Rather than put the metaphorical pillow over the head and try to ignore their existence, I wanted the children to feature as an integral part of this scheme. After all, they need to use this space too. As a result, the children pop up everywhere – from the roller blinds to life-size digi-print stickers on the wall – and are reassuringly never out of sight.

◆ *Painting a wall 148* ◆ *Making your own wallpaper with laser transfers 176* ◆ *Mosaic tiling 185* ◆ *Installing a roller blind 222* ◆

Toy story

The upholstered sleek-lined ottoman that forms the bed's footboard holds all the toys needed to distract these two on a Sunday morning. Notice also how it could effortlessly contain the pair of them – always a good threat. When closed it's the perfect viewing seat for DVD- or TV-viewing in plain parental sight at the end of the bed.

Tuck-away bathroom

The long and narrow layout of this space meant a well-appointed bathroom could be squeezed in behind the giant white leather headboard I'd conceived as a room divider. The space continues to feel uninterrupted and the black tiling in the bathroom serves to emphasise the whiteness of the sleeping area. A seamlessly integrated sliding door does give the option of privacy when needed.

For a lavish, luxurious guest-bedroom, I painted the walls to give way to a scenic panorama of idealised parkland. These are my variations on a very traditional design theme, playing with the decorating toys the aristocrats of our grandparents' generation so enjoyed.

Much of the cosy, country house grandeur in this room isn't what it seems. To start with, the proportions of the space itself have been bent and stretched. An unusually high-panelled dado rail helps increases the sense of vertical space within the room, whilst the pair of doors on either side of the bed help to create a sense of balance (one of these is actually a fake, there for just this reason) that this rather awkward layout would otherwise lack. Odd anomalies in the architecture from the slant of the roof above have been camouflaged within the mural, while the large window treatments with their attention-grabbing, red-lacquered pelmets also distract the eye away from the room's more awkard structural elements, encouraging us instead to see it as symmetrical and pleasingly in proportion. The wonderfully 'worn' tapestry used for the curtains and on the bed is actually a highly sophisticated, contemporary digi-print of an 18th-century French original that has been reproduced on soft linen. It is, if you like, a giant fabric photocopy. Meanwhile, of course, the belief that 'red and green should never be seen' is here joyously and unapologetically smashed into a million pieces. This is a room that wallows in the clichés of upper-class decorating confidence, while casually subverting any inbuilt snobbery with some highly theatrical techniques and a lot of contemporary materials.

28

*H*ouse guest heaven

Red and green can sometimes be seen

To paint a vista like this would have been impossible without green, but including it could have led to the typical complementary colour fight you get between these two colours – where red acts as a red rag to a green bull. To prevent this, rather than choose the brown-greens that one finds in nature (as you might have expected), I instead opted for a strong blue-green. My darkest green then became the colour for the woodwork. Having subtly turned the colour dial from green towards blue, I then picked a shade of red that errs towards orange. Now with the combative edge having been taken off both colours, both red and green can sit harmoniously together.

Extra-mural activities

Incorporating some scene painters' trickery into the design of this mural really helps give this space a sense of open perspective. Vanishing points have been concealed right in the corners of the room so that, as one views the painting from different angles, the rolling landscape appears to behave as a real, three-dimensional view would as it unfolds before the eye during a pleasant perambulation.

Trellage

To stop the dado panelling feeling a bit blank I designed some gothic-esque trellis which was laser-cut into thin MDF before being simply glued to the wall. This helps continue the Victorian-flavoured fiction that stems from the romantic, painted landscape above.

◆ Painting a wall 149 ◆ Painting woodwork 150 ◆ Upholstering a headboard 218 ◆ Making a pelmet 220 ◆ Hanging a curtain 223 ◆

What to do with weeny windows

As the ceiling in the room below this had previously been raised, the windows in this room are actually strangely low. To rebalance the funny proportions of this space I've made a huge theatrical fuss of the curtains, while linen blinds remain permanently lowered to hide the fact that the top of each window is, in reality, at hip height.

There's a fantastically unusual solution for a family like this one running out of room in the house. Build another one. And then link the two more or less identical structures with an open plan house height hall.

But how do you go about decorating such an extraordinary space? I don't know why I first thought Astroturf, but once in my brain it wasn't going to be shifted. I suppose it was something to do with the fact that this new internal area used to be outside but the practical benefits of fake grass in a high-impact, heavy-use area that offers the main access into the garden were an obvious consideration. The exciting first floor bridge that links the old house and the new build had obvious dramatic decorative potential from the outset. I designed an intricate fret of bent winter branches to undulate in a rather twiggy, Art Nouveau way from a central access. After a lot of deliberation I decided to have the pattern laser cut in grass green acrylic. When sunlight floods through the glass roof the translucent balustrade comes brilliantly alive and looks like a magically lit fairy tale thicket.

29

The hallway gallery

The call of the hall

Obviously this hallway is much more generous in its proportions than most, so being able to give it uses above and beyond being a straightforward transitional space is easy to envisage. But I'm a great believer in not letting a single cubic inch of our homes go to waste, so even in halls a fraction of the size of this one, I will often suggest placing an armchair or an occasional table. Okay, not many of us may have a compelling desire to go and sit in our halls, but isn't it nice to have the option should you suddenly desire to? Anyway, even if you don't have the time to stop and park your bottom on it as you whisk through, you do have a moment to stop and set your eyes on it on your journey from A to B.

In, out, shake it all about

Tough and practical, but soft and oddly comforting underfoot, the astroturf does a fabulous job of giving this inside space an outside vibe. It also (and here's a really serious domestic advantage) looks even better strewn with muddy footprints. But it's not just the floor that's feeling the call of the wild, in this hallway the walls are shiplap clad in the exact same white painted planking used to cover the outside surfaces. The subtle undulations of shade that light draws out from the wood grain create an ever-shifting wallpaper pattern, part contemporary design motif, part traditional garden shed.

Well hello Dali

The surrealism of this space is lost on no one. And it's not just the lawn floor, it's things like the floating art and empty picture frames that look as if they're framing a few yards of empty wall. It's no surprise to find ducks in here alongside art featuring repeating gerbils or exquisitely romantic dreamscape landscapes.

◆ *Painting a wall 148* ◆ *Painting woodwork 150* ◆ *Hanging a picture with a mirror plate 197* ◆ *Covering a lampshade with wallpaper 220* ◆

Tidy up time

Remembering back to when my two children were tiny, there always seemed to be a power struggle going on for ownership of the living room. Since grown-up spaces quickly become colonised by children's clutter, I had the idea of standing up against the tide of brightly coloured plastic by using cunning design to ensure that the living room can regain its grown-up credentials after a three-minute makeover.

In this room I had, like the interior design version of the UN, been called in to broker peace talks. During the day, Oliver holds sway and takes his responsibilities as mess-maker very seriously indeed. But after bath and bed time the living room needed to be able to become a grown-up zone where the responsibilities of child care could be gently eased with white wine and low lighting. Whilst quick, convenient and easily accessible storage solutions all help enormously, in this scheme my secret weapon for achieving this goal was my choice of colours. The tasteful layering of taupe linens and khakis creates a sophisticated framework onto which I spattered accent areas of bright orange, green, red and blue. Inspired by the invigorating palette of children's toys, the high-impact colour blocks help to soften the impact of kiddie clutter. Using lampshades, accessories and judiciously chosen art, I drip-fed the room with homeopathic qualities of bright accent colour. The careful blend of practicality and style means that there's something in this space for all the family.

30

Growing up quickly

Yes, it is the same room all grown-up. Thanks to a little help from Oliver, all the toys have now been put to bed in their window seat storage dormitories, which handily double as additional banquette seating, for when there are visiting adults around. Meanwhile the chairs have been pulled around an open bottle of wine and the candles in the hearth have been lit. In this atmospheric, sultry light the room really does feel like an entirely different, far more grown-up place to be.

Pretty practicality

Practicality doesn't necessarily have to mean sacrificing stylish design. In this room, vertical lines create a visual texture that helps to knit the various colours and themes of this design scheme together. Even the slots of the radiator covers, which keeps little fingers away from hot surfaces, rhyme. On the floor a 'rug' of carpet tiles is the perfect surface for push cars. And, should a cup of juice go awry, then the stained tile can simply be lifted from its companions and replaced with a nice new one.

Safety first

The pretty little lamps on the mantelpiece are plugged into 5 amp sockets just below the shelf that are turned on and off from a switch at the door. Placing the sockets deliberately and discreetly high means that there are no trailing cables for inquisitive little hands to tug at. Lighting the room with wall lights as opposed to lamps meanwhile ensures that there are no flexes for little hands and mouths to get hold of.

◆ *Painting stripes 159* ◆ *Painting woodwork 150* ◆ *Hanging a mirror 196* ◆ *Laying carpet tiles 204* ◆

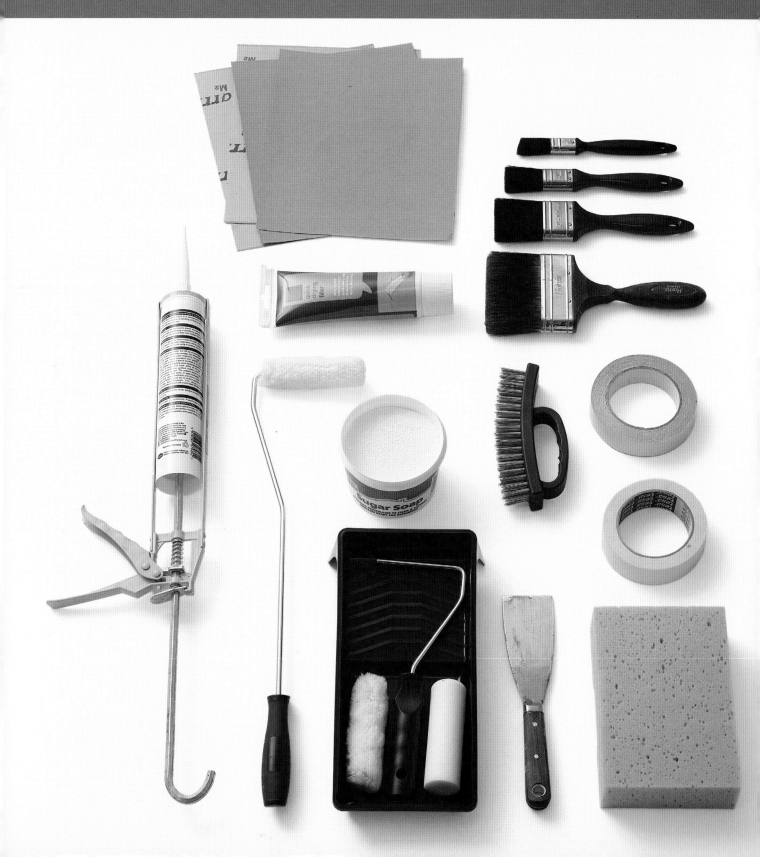

PAINTING

CLEANING A SURFACE FOR PAINTING

Although paint these days has been formulated to go successfully on top of most surfaces, you really don't want dust or muck trapped underneath a permanent coating of emulsion. Besides, there's something about preparing a surface for painting that can't help but put you in the right frame of mind for decorating.

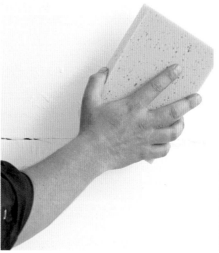

1. Mix some sugar soap into a warm-ish bucket of water. It's tough stuff, so don't overdo the formulation. Sugar soap is perfect for cutting through emulsion's arch-enemy – grease.

2. Use a sponge and some elbow grease to wipe over the surface of whatever you're wanting to paint. Start high and work your way down. This means you won't be dripping onto finished bits.

3. Make sure the surface is dry before you start any plastering, filling or painting. A dry duster or dishcloth is perfect for getting rid of any excess moisture that may still be on the surface.

PLASTERING

Areas of plaster or old paint that are loose or a bit wobbly need to be addressed before you can even think about starting painting.

1. I always find a wire brush is great for exfoliating away surface flaky bits. Be brave - it's best that anything unstable parts company from the surface at the outset.

2. Now wash the surface down with a water/sugar soap solution to get rid of any dusty leftovers.

3. Abrading the surface will often leave exposed areas of raw plaster which might cause problems later on. I'll often use watery PVA glue to seal recently deflaked areas and ready them for painting.

FILLING

Modern fillers dry astonishingly quickly and can be sanded down to an almost invisible state. Spend time applying them well and you'll save yourself time sanding and fiddling around later.

1. Always use a filler blade. Here I've squirted a generous blob of ready-mixed quick-drying filler ready to go.

2. Rather like icing a cake, go for swift, maximum coverage at the outset – literally filling the area with little concern for style.

3. Now for the finesse. Positioning the filler blade's edge at right angles to the surface, scrape the excess filler off the areas where it's not required.

4. Doing it properly at first should mean there's little sanding to do afterwards. But don't forget, if you're not happy with filler attempt number one, you can always go again until you are.

HEAVY FILLING

Really scary holes and cracks might well need professional plastering. Big filling jobs need a 'tough love, make it worse before making it better' attitude.

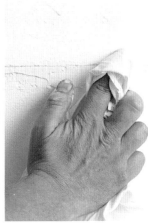

1. Scrape out the hole or crack first, ensuring anything loose or unstable bites the dust.

2. Premixed decorator's caulk is a godsend for big jobs. It's wonderfully rubbery and can cover quite significant holes or cracks.

3. Once you've applied a good-enough amount to roughly fill the area, use a filler blade at right angles to the wall to flatten off the rubbery goo.

4. You may find a dampish cloth useful to smooth the healing wound off further before it sets for good.

PAINTING PREPARATION

Painting a room yourself can be good, clean honest fun. The secret is to relax and enjoy the process. Don't let yourself get anxious or het up and, whatever you do, for goodness sake please don't rush it.

1. It's essential you mix paint well before you start. If you're not careful, blobs of pigment will make their way from tin to wall if not properly stirred in. I like to start with a good shake - obviously making sure the lid's on tight first!

2. Open the lid with a screwdriver, easing it away gently and making sure you don't bend the lip of the lid back. Little flicks moving gently around the edge are better than a single wrench.

3. Use a stick or, best of all, a wooden spoon to give the paint a good old stir. Go on, get right down to the gooey bits at the bottom of the tin.

4. Now take a clean, dry, good-quality paintbrush, holding its handle just above the brush bit itself.

5. Dip the brush into the centre of the tin, ensuring that you don't get any paint on the handle. Load the bristles until they are heavy with paint.

6. Finally remove the gloopy excess stuck on the outside of the bristles by dragging the sides of the brush over the edge of the tin.

PAINTING A WALL

I always like to start my painting off at eye level. There are plenty who say you should start with the top of the wall or do the 'cutting in' (the edges) first, but I like to treat myself to a nice big block of colour to start with to get me in the painting mood.

1. Hold your brush gently. If you grasp it too hard you'll soon tire yourself out, get hideous cramp and not enjoy the experience. I've always found a loose grip rather like holding a pencil works brilliantly.

2. Allow the paint to do the work for you. Keep the brush strokes going in energetic criss-crosses until the wall begins to change colour.

3. As you go along, make sure you smooth out large blobs or clots of paint, evening the surface out as you go.

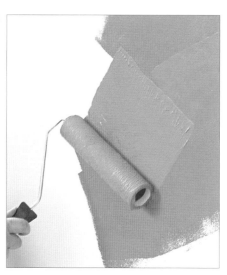

4. When using a roller, start by pouring plenty of paint into the roller tray reservoir. Then use the roller to roll an even layer across the surface of the roll out area.

5. It's important that your roller is as evenly covered with paint as possible. So roll it backwards and forwards. I'll often give it a couple of passes at right angles just to make sure the colour has been spread evenly.

6. Now attack the wall. Beware little clods and 'snots' (an old decorating term, don't you know), the little bits of drying paint or dust that can get stuck in the wet surface.

PAINTING WOODWORK

There was a time when painting woodwork with smelly, slow-drying oil paints was a fastidious job requiring sanding between coats, patience and a lot of sighing. Luckily, modern acrylic-based woodwork paints make this once-thankless task much, much easier.

1. Assuming you've swottishly done all your surface preparation (see pages 146-7), start the ball rolling by using a roughish bristled brush to paint the surrounding architraves.

2. Now attack any panel mouldings. My tip is to use quite a heavily laden brush to both apply the paint and smooth out the surface as you go.

3. Keep your brush strokes going in the same direction for an equally balanced, consistent finish.

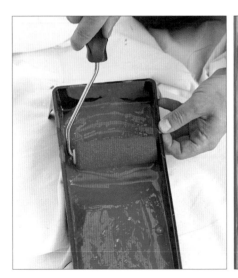

4. Now for the clever bit, a small hard foam roller. This is the best thing I know for creating a smooth, lacquer-like finish. Pour plenty of paint into the tray and use the roller to spread it out.

5. With glossy or eggshell paints it's extremely important that the paint gets uniformly applied to the roller. So take a little time to roll, roll, roll and re-roll in the roll out section of the tray.

6. Then crack on, keeping the roller strokes going in one direction. Don't even try to do it in one go. Resign yourself to a two- or three-coater to get the best possible finish.

CLEANING PAINT BRUSHES AND ROLLERS

There are those who go for a disposable brush regime when decorating – buying them cheap and then chucking them once the job is done. I can't bring myself to do this. I love soft, shiny-bristled paint brushes and sturdy rollers and I'm prepared to look after them.

1. Clean off the worst of the paint with newspaper – I find it has just the right tough love properties to take off any excess paint cleanly.

2. Apply washing-up liquid straight to the bristles, dip the paint brush quickly into a bucket of water and then lather.

3. Focus particular attention at the roots of the bristles where the paint can accumulate. For very posh brushes (like dragging or lining brushes that cost a small fortune) I might even use conditioner. Rinse and repeat until the water runs clear.

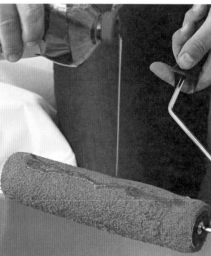

4. To clean your roller, start by rolling the worst of the paint out onto newspaper until the roller strokes become ghostly.

5. Now trickle washing up liquid straight onto the roller sleeve before wetting in a bucket of water.

6. Beware, rollers are messy!. Prepare to get stuck in and treat the roller sleeve like a dangerously muddy sausage dog that's likely to shake everywhere after a bath.

STORING PAINT BRUSHES AND ROLLERS

There's nothing worse than constantly having to buy bits anew simply because you can't find (or you hadn't correctly stored) what you already own.

1. To keep a brush fresh enough for use over a lunch break, wrap it tightly in an airtight sheath of cling film to avoid having to wash it out.

2. The same goes for roller sleeves. An airtight sandwich bag or carrier bag does more or less the same job. Don't be tempted to leave wrapped rollers or brushes for more than a few hours, however, or they will dry out.

3. Paint already poured into a roller tray can be kept fresh and usable under cling film. Be prepared to remove a custard skin of paint from the surface if you leave it like this for more than a long-ish sandwich break.

STORING A PAINT TIN

When you've got ranks of more or less identical cans stacked in a shed, finding the right colour once the label's dropped off can be a nightmare. Try storing them like this to save pain later.

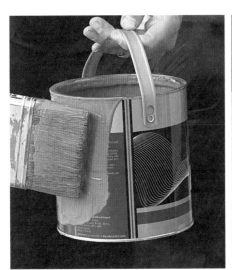

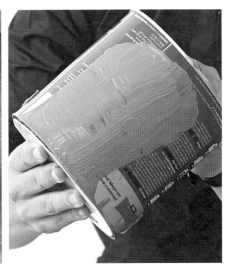

1. I always apply a nice big patch of paint to the side of the tin so that the colour's easily visible.

2. Make sure you get that lid back on nice and tight. You should feel a click all the way around as you apply pressure.

3. Provided the lid's on properly, I store my paint upside down. This means that the inevitable crust which forms over the surface of the stored paint occurs at the bottom of the tins and not the top. This means the paint is ready to go when I need it. Clever.

RETINTING PAINT

Getting paint home and finding it's wrong happens to the best of us every now and again. Most of the time it's because the colour's too bright or too fruity. Don't despair, I have a solution...

1. Pour a third of the offending shade out into a paint kettle and set the rest aside.

2. Mix up a remedial tint using a suitable acrylic paint. I use complementary colour theory to tone down a tone I don't like. If a red is too bright, I'll use green or if a blue is too blue, I'll pick orange. But a good catch-all solution is a Raw Umber, which is a great natural brown.

3. Take a nice big blob of acrylic and mix it with water, being careful to ensure all the little bits of undissolved pigment combine with the liquid.

4. Keep stirring until you have a coloured suspension with a consistency that could best be described as 'gravy-like'.

5. Pour the coloured suspension into the kettle in which you've put the third of the tin of paint. I will usually stir the paint at the same time to ensure an even mix.

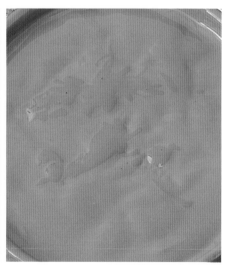

6. To assess the change, return a few discreet blobs of the retinted paint onto the surface of the unmixed colour. Should your new shade have gone too far, the two-thirds you held back can then be called upon to rebalance the mix.

REMOVING PAINT STAINS

Accidents happen to the best of us. When they do, swift action is the key – try to soak up as much as possible with absorbent kitchen towel or, if the worst comes to the worst, newspaper.

1. Dried in blobs or spots of paint on the carpet aren't in fact the end of the world. Use a sharp scalpel to gently scrape them away.

2. Keep the blade at a right angle to the carpet pile and gently stroke the scalpel sharp edge over the dried paint.

3. Work slowly and methodically to remove the paint-clogged ends of the carpet pile.

4. On clothes, I've found the most efficient tool in the paint removal armoury to be the baby wipe.

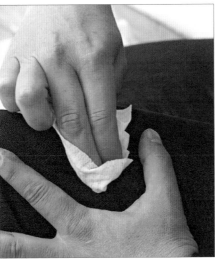

5. They can, I completely assure you, take even quite hardened paint out of the weave of fabric with a consistent, no-nonsense application.

6. With such wonderful paint solvent abilities, I've often wondered whether, after prolonged use, baby wipes might not eventually dissolve babies...

PAINTING STRIPES

Painting stripes on a wall is, if you like, the nursery slope of specialist paint finishing. Its simplicity, however, is not apparent from the finished effect.

1. Use a spirit level to measure out your stripe lines. I find it's a good idea to sketch up where you want the stripes on a piece of paper first.

2. Use low-tack masking tape to create a crisp edge to paint to. My tip is to put the edge of the tape just the other side of the pencil line that you have measured to ensure it gets painted out.

3. Now take a well-loaded paint brush and start filling the stripes in.

4. I always find that painting over the taped edges is best done when the brush has less paint on it. So, build up a pattern where you start the painting in the middle first and leave the edges until last.

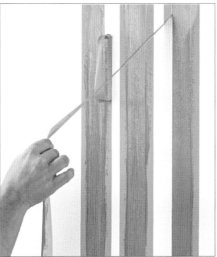

5. I find leaving tape on for too long can cause problems, so when the paint is dry-ish (about 10-15 minutes) peel it off carefully.

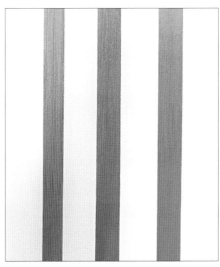

6. As you get better at this technique, why not try applying the paint so that the stripes retain a slight brushed texture – this can look wonderful.

A TROMPE L'OEIL PANEL

A trompe l'oeil panel works best if you pick three closely related shades. When choosing your mid-tone wall colour, buy a little tin of the darker and lighter shades either side of it for just this purpose.

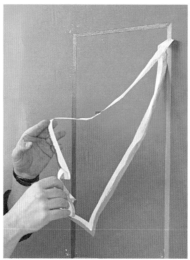

1. Using a spirit level and a nice, sharp pencil, mark out your panel, having measured out the size, shape and distance between each side with a tape measure.

2. Use low-tack masking tape to mask out the outside edge. If you're really clever, get the edge of the tape so that it leaves the pencil line visible.

3. Then mask out an inner line approximately one centimetre away. This will be the bit you put the paint in, so having the pencil line between the two tapes ensures it gets painted out.

4. Neaten up the internal corners with a craft knife. The effect relies on a nice, crisp edge, so make sure there aren't any stray bits of tape.

5. Look at how the light hits the room. Paint one side and the top in the darker shade to match with what would cast a shadow in real life.

6. Use the light colour on the opposite side and on the bottom. Where the two colours meet, paint in a diagonal line to help give the panel that little extra illusion of real depth.

7. Peel the tape off slowly. It's a good idea to take the tape off when the paint is dryish – 10 to 15 minutes is fine but beware as it can get a little less than low-tack if it stays in one place too long.

8. Be prepared to touch up any little areas of damaged paintwork where the tape has pulled flecks of colour off.

MIXING SCUMBLE GLAZE

Scumble is one of decorating's most flavourful words. At its most basic, scumble creates a light, see-through veil of coloured paint that takes a long time to dry. There is, however, a lot more fun to be had with scumble, as the following four techniques demonstrate.

1. Pour your glaze, in quantities according to the manufacturer's instructions, into a paint kettle.

2. Add either coloured emulsion paint or acrylic pigment into the waiting glaze.

3. Stir well, remembering that the acrylic glaze's 'white when wet' rule will make your colour glaze look chalky in the pot.

4. Try a bit on your chosen surface and see how it dries before making a final decision. Meanwhile, stir, stir and stir again to ensure your glaze is well and truly mixed together.

COLOUR WASHING

 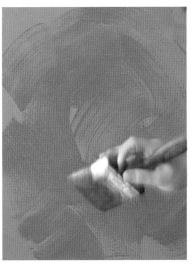  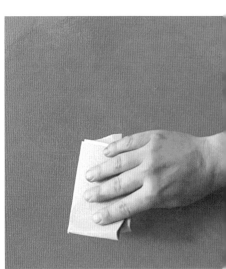

1. Apply the tinted scumble using a big, soft emulsion brush. I always favour a series of large, semicircular strokes.

2. Whilst it's all still wet and gooey, apply more strokes in an opposite direction to build up an abstract, cloudy effect.

3. Now use a soft cotton rag (beware of unravelling edges that might get caught in the sticky glaze) to soften the strokes into vaporous patches.

4. When dry, further subtlety can be added by sanding lightly with coarse-grain sandpaper. This is also very useful if you find dark patches where different applications of paint have gone on top of each other.

DRAGGING

Scumbling can create a myriad of soft, naturalistic textures for bringing a wall to life. Dragging is a very traditional finish that works particularly well in high-ceilinged rooms.

1. Apply a nice, generous colour glaze in a broad stripe and brush it around to ensure that there are no thick blobs or thin patches.

2. Starting at the top and going down to the bottom, firmly pull an ordinary plastic comb through the gooey glaze.

3. The effect should be of a soft, almost cloth-like vertical texture.

SPONGING

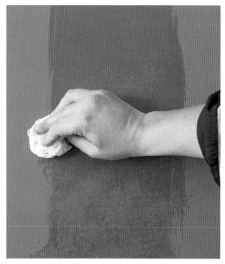

1. Apply the colour glaze in approximately 30cm wide panels, evening the surface out as you go so it's well distributed.

2. Using a natural sponge, press firmly on the colour glaze to create pitted blotches that should look a bit like an open-grained wood.

3. A good tip is to constantly keep turning the sponge – reversing it, swapping it and rotating it so that you avoid leaving the same obvious print.

RAGGING

Ragging is a very, very old decorative technique that can be traced back to the Renaissance. The imprinted surface creates a fractured, crystalline finish that can look almost marble-like.

1. Start by applying a much thicker, even layer of scumble glaze on the wall than you would for the other scumble glaze techniques.

2. Take a cotton cloth (beware stray threads that might get stuck) and gently leave soft impressions in the wet glaze. Turn the cloth regularly to avoid obvious repeats.

3. Alternatively, try using polythene bags, cling film, or greaseproof paper in place of the cotton cloth in order to achieve different patterns and effects.

WOODGRAINING

 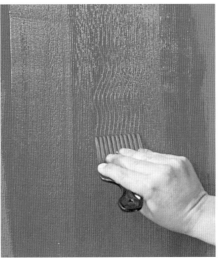 

1. My technique for simple woodgraining uses a pair of cheap plastic combs. After applying the scumble glaze as you would for dragging, use an ordinary fine-toothed comb to leave delicate vertical lines in the glaze.

2. Now, and here comes the clever bit, use a much broader-toothed comb, like an afro comb, moving it slowly from side to side as you pull down to give a wavy suggestion of woodgrain.

3. Whilst still wet, the effect can be made more subtle by being gently brushed over in the direction of the grain using a soft, dry paint brush.

STENCILLING

Stencilling has to be just about the most ancient way of cheering up a surface. The Egyptians were great stencil enthusiasts – as a technique it suited their taste in repeating patterns perfectly.

 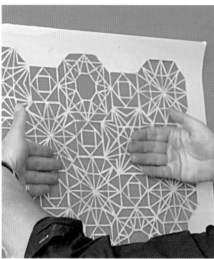 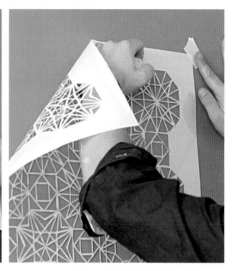

1. Stencil card is the traditional choice for stencillers. It's quite thick stuff and smells wonderfully oily. Personally, however, I prefer acetate, which when cut is thin enough to create a crisp stenciled outline.

2. I use non-permanent, repositionable spray adhesive to hold the stencil in place. Give it a good even squirt and then let it dry a bit – it actually gets tackier the longer you leave it – before sticking it to your surface.

3. Fixing little squares of masking tape to the corners of the stencil is a good way of making sure it doesn't float away once you've started working on it.

STENCILLING WITH A BRUSH

1. Using a short, stubby brush, apply a little paint through the stencil.

2. Try to use as little paint as possible – notice how I've blobbed excess paint from the brush onto the uncut part of the stencil.

3. When removing the stencil from your surface, peel it off gently or else you'll risk damaging, ripping or stretching it.

4. To add a sense of depth or volume to the motif, try varying the density of the paint in certain areas.

STENCILLING WITH SPRAY PAINT

Using spray paint has the benefit of providing a more uniform finish than brushing, but the disadvantage is a lot of extra preparation. You'll also need a mask to stave off those horrid fumes.

1. Don't underestimate how far your spray will spray. Use newspaper to create a decently doughty mask around the stencil.

2. Spray your stencil slowly and carefully. Don't be seduced by speed to blitz the poor stencil with high-energy blasts of paint. It'll only trickle if you do.

3. Spray paint dries quickly, so additional colours or (as here) metallics can be added to make decorative effects.

4. This mosaic style motif looks particularly good with flashes of old gold highlighting the bright pink.

VARNISH STENCILLING

Using a traditional damask motif stencil you can create your own posh wallpaper – not by using a contrasting or coordinating colour, but by bringing in a bit of shine instead.

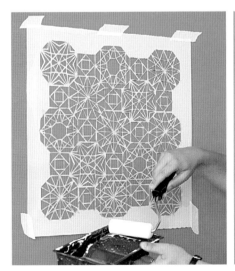  

1. As what you're about to do will take your stencil to its very limits, fix it in place securely before pouring quick-drying gloss acrylic varnish into a small, hard-foam roller tray.

2. Ensure the roller is not overloaded with varnish, but has a nice even coat by rollering it back and forth in the tray. Apply the varnish in gentle passes, regularly changing directions to even it out.

3. Be particularly gentle when removing the varnish-drenched stencil from the wall to avoid smudging or ruining the pattern.

WALLPAPERING

APPLYING WALLPAPER

Of all the jolly jobs in the pantheon of decorating, I've always found wallpapering to be the most satisfying. Having said this, it's perfectly normal to view the paper in its tight roll and the wall in its naked, unpapered state with trepidation. Put the preparation time in working it out first, however, and you will learn to love it too.

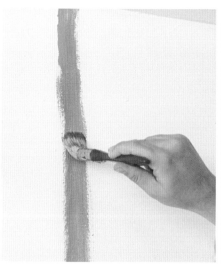

1. Wallpapering isn't, I'm afraid, one of those projects on which you hit the deck running. Start by finding the middle of the wall and then hold up a roll of paper. Mark where its ends come and use a spirit level to give you a line to follow. Don't start in a corner and work out, as corners are rarely true enough to be trusted.

2. Carry on across the wall, measuring where each roll will end and drawing a spirit level line. Next, using a dark-ish or midtone colour from the paper's pattern, paint over each of the vertical 'seam' lines where the paper will join itself.

3. Colour in the end of the roll using a permanent-ink felt tip marker. This is a bit of an optional extra, but it does help if you've got dark, big-patterned paper which might betray itself with a pale paper edge at the seam line when stuck on the wall.

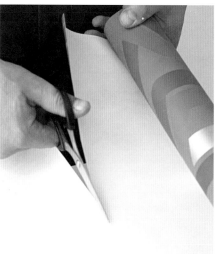

4. Measure out your first 'drop' (length) of wallpaper. At this stage it's worth holding the paper up in position to work out where the pattern's going to crop up. It may even be worth positioning a motif in a particular spot which you'll be able to do at this stage but not later.

5. Now cut your wallpaper length out, allowing a good 30cm or so overhang at top and bottom.

6. Next paste the wall. Yes, the wall. I always use a roller which gives you the most even coverage. Pasting the wall ensures that the adhesive is less likely to soak in and create wrinkles or bubbles in the finished effect. Use a two-thirds to one-third diluted formula of wallpaper paste. Allow the wall to almost competely dry.

7. Again using a roller, paste the paper with full-strength adhesive. Get the glue right up to the edges, which is where it is needed most.

8. As you go along, fold the paper against itself pattern side to pattern side which will give you an easy-to-manage bundle. Then let it stand. I always think in terms of letting a bundle stand for the time it takes me to paste up the next bundle.

9. Now it's sticky time. Be patient at this point. Position the paper from the top, ensuring the edge follows the vertical spirit level line on the wall. Gently move the paper to and fro using the flats of both your hands until it's more or less where you want it.

10. With a dry wallpaper brush, start brushing the paper flat, smoothing out wrinkles and bubbles as you go. Little pouches nearly always dry out on their own, so focus on the big eye-catching imperfections.

11. Clean off any excess adhesive or fingerprints with a damp sponge on the edge of dryness.

12. Trim away excess paper with a painfully sharp knife and metal straight edge. Then be brave! When soggy, the wallpaper will look shocking but – trust me – after 20 minutes once it has dried off it will be reincarnated as a perfectly papered wall.

13. Get on with the next bits. Match up the pattern on your next drop up to its newly installed neighbour. Ensure you've got your 30cm overhang at top and bottom before cutting your drop to your requirements.

14. Cut and paste as before. When positioning the new drop, make sure you start with a matched pattern first before you stick it in its final position.

WALLPAPERING AROUND CORNERS

The current and continuing vogue for papering one wall is, I believe, something of a missed opportunity. For those who would like to paper further but worry about encountering obstacles like corners in the process, let the following reassure you. It's really not that difficult.

1. When you get to a corner, you'll see yourself how important it is not to trust them. Even in newish houses they're rarely straight. So, measure up and mark up as you go.

2. At the corner, make sure the pattern mark is perfectly aligned and the seam between the drop lengths is discreetly buffed before attempting to bend the paper. With gentle horizontal movements, coax the paper into and over the corner.

3. Use a dry brush to get the paper as tight into the corner as possible.

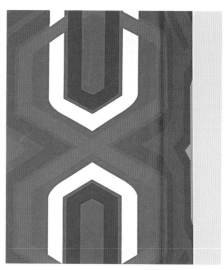

4. Resist the temptation to prod or poke at the paper, since at this stage it's at its most fragile. A soft dry brush and firm patience work wonders.

5. If the going is getting tough, it's because the paper is drying out. Keep the paper a little moist (and therefore pliable) with a damp sponge.

6. I always find the best finishing touch to be a final flourish right down the corner from top to bottom with a damp sponge, just to crispen and neaten up the geometry.

WALLPAPERING AROUND A LIGHT SWITCH

Professionals will probably pooh-pooh this but, for safety reasons, I'm not very keen to encourage anyone to take a light switch or socket off the wall. Besides, though it may be a little more fiddly, it is actually not a bad discipline to learn how to work around intrusive objects.

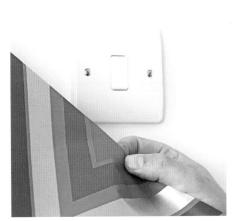

1. Cut your length of wallpaper to fit the wall as before. Then offer it up to the wall, as straight as you can, right over the offending switch.

2. Now use a pencil to mark the four corners of the switch as accurately as you can.

3. Lay the length flat on a work surface and, using a craft knife, cut along the line that would diagonally connect the four pencil marks, leaving a centimetre or so at the end of the line before you get to the pencil marks themselves. This allows you a bit of leeway when the paper goes up.

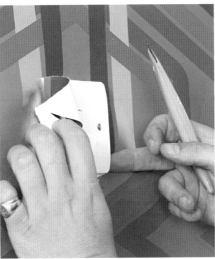

4. Paste and install the paper as usual. Concentrate on getting the pattern match right and smoothing out crinkles or wrinkles before you begin to worry about the switch.

5. Ideally the cuts you've made in the paper won't completely expose the switch. This means you'll need to extend them to allow the switch to completely poke through.

6. To finish, trim away the excess using your craft knife following the outside edge of the switch.

COVERING A SHELF WITH WALLPAPER

This is something I like to do a lot. Wallpaper is surprisingly hardwearing and will withstand regular (but not heavy-duty) use as a shelf finish. Papering your shelves to match the wall means that the eye can feast on what the shelves display, without the visual distraction of the shelf itself.

1. Using an off-the-shelf shelf kit, abrade the factory finish with coarse sandpaper to create a key for the adhesive.

2. Next mark out the shelf's outline onto the back of the wallpaper, taking care to position the pattern on the right side of the shelf.

3. Cut diagonals at each corner to make folding in excess paper easier when you stick the paper on the shelf.

4. Apply heavy-duty wallpaper adhesive to the paper with a foam roller. Ready-mixed border and repair adhesive is ideally suited to this project.

5. Stick the paper over the shelf, constantly smoothing out wrinkles and lumps and bumps as you go.

6. Fold the corners in and then trim off the waste with the sharpest of sharp knives.

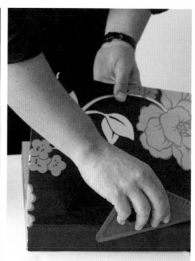

7. Use a straight edge with great care and tact to smooth down the paper and ensure it clings crisply to the shelf.

8. Trim off anything left overlapping on the back edge of the shelf that will butt up to the wall.

APPLYING WALLPAPER IN PANELS

Cutting decorative shapes in patterned wallpaper and then sticking them in regular intervals straight onto the wall is a great way of creating a grand panelled feel economically.

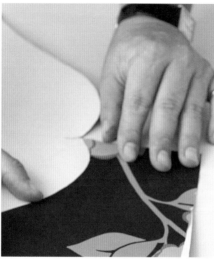

1. Mark out half a glamorous panel shape to the top of the paper you wish to use and cut it with a sharp pair of scissors.

2. Fold the paper panel in half down a vertical centre line so that the top edges of the paper coincide in a perfect geometrical line.

3. Trace the profile of the cut shape onto the uncut half of the paper to make a beautifully symmetrical 'Butterfly' match. Cut out the shape.

4. Paste using heavy-duty paste or border and repair adhesive, taking care to get into the corners. This is important because the edges of your shape must not be easy to peel off or susceptible to damage

5. Stick the wallpaper up as before. Pay particular attention to excess adhesive that might escape the edge and mark the wall.

6. Repeat using the same shape in a careful rhythm. A good tip is to pre-mark a vertical line with a spirit level for each panel position to work to.

STRIPPING WALLPAPER

Taking down wallpaper is often thought of as an onerous and tricky task. It's not in fact. The secret is to get between the wall and the wallpaper with as much moisture as possible.

1. I've found over the years that one of the best ways of starting off is to close all the windows and doors and keep boiling a kettle in the room until the steam really builds up.

2. Encourage the paper off the wall by gently scoring it using a sharp knife. Be careful not to scratch the plaster below. This will help encourage the steam to get in behind the paper

3. Either use a wallpaper steamer or an old-fashioned sponge to get behind the wallpaper through the slashed weak points. The wetter the paper becomes, the easier it is to remove.

4. Now gently coax small pieces of paper away from the walls using a wallpaper stripping blade or a flat spatula.

5. A good tip is to start with the weakest points, like the joins between wallpaper drops or the top or bottom edges pf the paper.

6. Don't be greedy. Keep the bits you scrape off small. Large, heavy lumps of paper pulled by overexcited fingers may very well dislodge bits of wall plaster.

MAKING YOUR OWN WALLPAPER WITH LASER TRANSFERS

Computers are wonderfully clever things and I've quite fallen in love with their ability to print out any motif onto transfer paper which can then go straight onto the wall (or even onto a cushion cover, as pictured here).

1. Take your chosen print and cut around the edge of the printed transfer paper to give a reasonable idea of their finished shape, before roughly positioning them using masking tape.

2. Once happy with your transfer's intended position, lift up your transfer and apply slightly diluted PVA adhesive to overlap the shape. If you use a roller it will be less likely to bubble or dribble.

3. Remove the paper transfer from the wall and leave the PVA to become tacky but not too dry. Remember that PVA dries clear, so as long as you can still see its opaque whiteness, you're all right.

4. Pop the transfer into a bucket of water and wait for it to curl into a roll.

5. Now delicately position the transfer on the wall over the tacky PVA and stealthily slide the backing paper away.

6. Use a dry sponge to flatten out bubbles and, when it's all dry, finish the job by coating the wall in a quick-drying acrylic varnish.

TILING

TILING

Terrible tiling and grotty grouting can really make bath times a bore. In fact, sorting out tiles can be really very rewarding – an ideal Saturday afternoon job you should finish just in time for an evening bath treat.

1. Mark out the area you are intending to tile using a spirit level. Never trust a corner, skirting or a ceiling to do this job for you. Mark out a vertical centre line in the middle of this tiling area.

2. Now measure out how many tiles you'll need to travel the distance you'll need to get up the wall. Be prepared to add 3mm to each tile dimension to accommodate grout.

3. Lay your first line of tiles along the floor, starting with one in the middle whose centre line corresponds with the vertical centre line you've already marked on the wall. This will also demonstrate where you'll need to cut tiles. It's best to keep tiles that need to be cut to discreet positions in the corners of the room.

4. Now get messy with it. Splodge tile adhesive straight onto the wall in as consistent a thick old coat as you can get. Use a tile spreader to distribute the goo in many lines; this will help the tiles stick better.

5. Since you're starting from the skirting, snip one limb of the cross-shaped tile spacers.

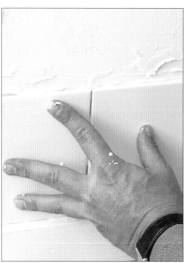

6. Start tiling, using the spacers you've cut down from crosses into upside down 'T's. The spacers are essential for creating a crisp effect, so take time to get them right.

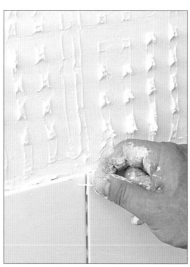

7. Start building up your tiling course on course with spacers at every junction between the tiles. Keep checking your tiles with a spirit level to ensure your tiling isn't sliding off on a diagonal.

8. Wipe off any oozed or spilt adhesive before it has a chance to dry. Now step back and leave the tile adhesive to dry out thoroughly.

GROUTING AND SILICONE EDGING

At this pre-grouted stage your tiling may very well all look a bit ragged, but don't despair. Once the grout comes out and the edging has been applied it will all look wonderfully professional.

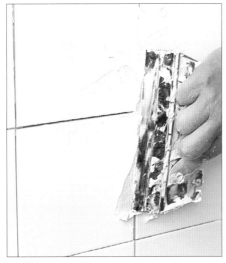

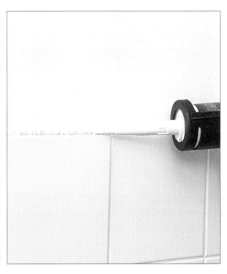

1. Check everything's stuck firmly down before applying your grout with enthusiastic scrapes or a rubber-edged grout trowel. Take time to really force it into the gaps and then, keeping the trowel at a right angle to the tiling, scrape off the waste to instantly neaten up the effect.

2. Now take a semi-damp sponge and wipe across the tiled area to bring the gleam of the tile up through the powdery grout.

3. When applying silicone as finishing or damp proofing, try to keep consistent pressure onto the pump so that the line of silicone remains as free of big blobs as possible.

4. To finish and neaten the silicone there really is no beating a lightly licked finger.

5. Drag your ever-so-slightly-damp digit across the silicone line in one smooth consistent motion to smooth the silicone and clean off any excess..

6. If finishing the silicone goes a bit awry, don't panic. Simply wait for it to be thoroughly dry before cutting back any splurges with a sharp knife.

CUTTING TILES

There is, it has to be conceded, something rather nerve-wracking about cutting tiles to size. Until confidence is gained, I always advise a quick practice with an already broken tile.

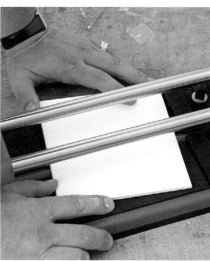

1. Measure out where you intend to cut your tile carefully and use a soft-ish pencil to make a mark on its porous, unglazed edge.

2. Position the tile in a tile cutter, making sure the cutting wheel and your measure mark coincide.

3. Apply pressure to the cutting wheel handle. You'll find a positioning, steadying aluminium 'foot' will come down to fix the tile in place and stop it from wiggling around.

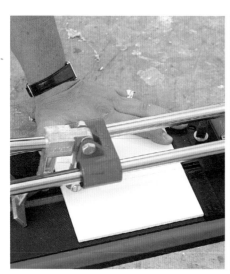

4. Draw the cutting wheel across the tile in a decisive, forthright manner. Resist the temptation to do this more than once. Honestly, it will have worked the first time.

5. The tile has now been fatally scored and, when the weak-point score line is placed over a straight edge and pressure is applied to either side – hey presto, snap.

6. Finish the raw edge off by smoothing it down with some wet-and-dry abrasive sanding paper.

REMOVING A TILE

When you've got one tile that's cracked, damaged or (as in this case) just plain ugly, it's not really necessary to condemn the whole wall. This technique will show you how to remove and replace the offending tile, leaving the remainder intact.

1. Use ordinary masking tape to cover the offending tile from corner to corner.

2. Then using an electric drill with a ceramic bit, drill a hole through the point where the masking tape crosses. Using the masking tape line ensures the drill has something to catch on to and should prevent it from skidding.

3. Now it's time to shatter the tile under controlled conditions by hitting a narrow screwdriver into the centre hole by its end with a hammer.

4. Now use the screwdriver to flick out the remaining chunks of the offending tile.

5. Clean the 'wound', by scraping off the old dried adhesive and scratching out the raggedy grout.

6. To finish, apply fresh adhesive and install a new, undamaged (or at least marginally better-looking) replacement tile.

TILING OVER TILES

If you've got a really deeply horrible wall full of tiles – possibly in some unspeakably hideous 1970s shade – please don't despair. You can tile over tiles (even ugly ones).

1. Gently scuff up the shiny surface of the ceramic tiles using wet-and-dry abrasive sanding paper.

2. Now, as though you were icing a Christmas cake, apply a fabulously generous layer of tile adhesive to the gently scuffed tiles.

3. Of course, having tiles on the wall already means you have a grid system to follow, so you don't really need to mark one out afresh.

4. Leave the adhesive to harden slightly for a few minutes before firmly applying the new tiles.

5. When applying each additional row of tiles, make sure that the spacers are correctly positioned between the tiles.

6. Leave the adhesive to dry thoroughly before grouting. Since the adhesive doesn't back onto a porous surface like plaster, the tiles behind will hold back the drying time as the moisture in it evaporates, so be patient.

MOSAIC TILING

For something that looks so fiddly, mosaic's actually quite easy to apply as it comes these days in meshed sheets. Something, I'm sure, that the Ancient Romans' mosaic slaves would no doubt have been highly jealous of.

1. With a sharp knife, slit the mosaic sheet mesh to pop out a number of mosaic tiles at random or in a pattern, depending on your design. These individual tiles are called tessarae.

2. Use a very fine-toothed adhesive spreader to apply an even, thickish layer of tile adhesive to your surface.

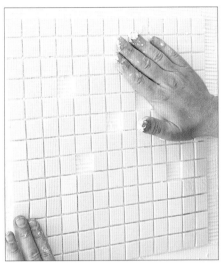

3. Position the mosaic on the surface rather like wallpaper, using the flats of your hands to coax it into position and resisting the temptation to pull, jerk or tug.

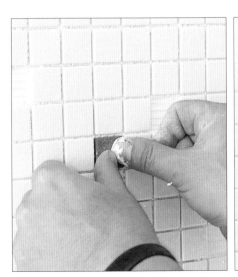

4. Replace the tessarae that had been removed with tiles of contrasting colours or finishes such as glass or metallic tiles.

5. Grout as with ordinary tiling, ensuring it gets deep down in between each tessara.

6. Finish by evening the grout off and removing any excess with a slightly damp sponge.

WOODWORKING

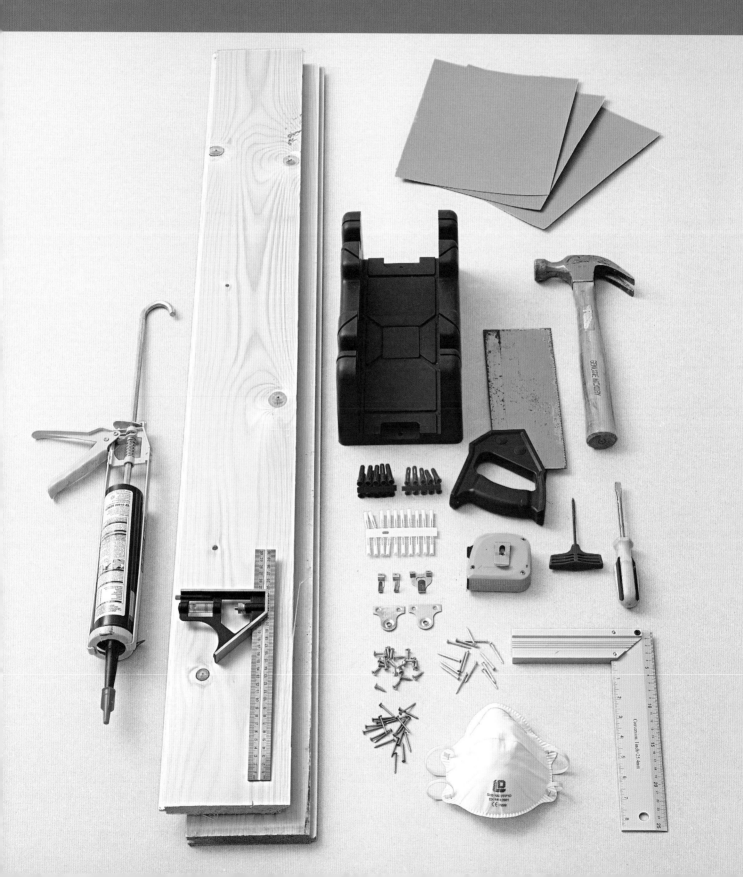

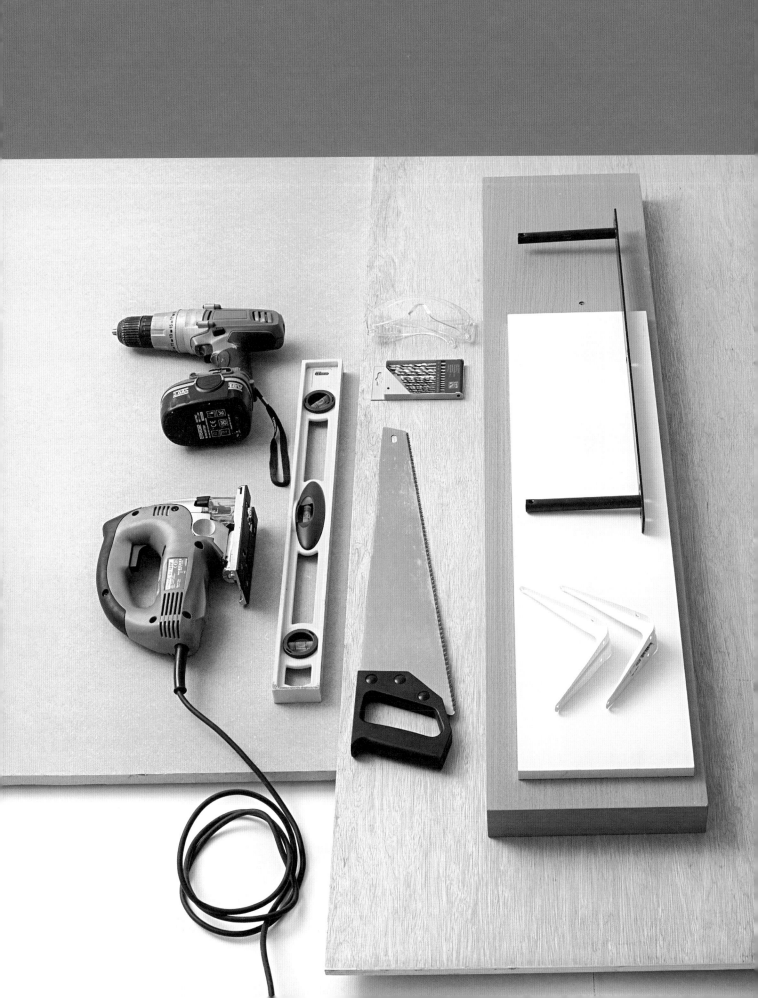

BASIC NAILING

I've found over the years that there's an almost entirely infallible way of nailing that, I'm happy to guarantee, won't result in bruised thumbs.

1. Hold the nail steady at its very end so that the finger and thumb create a cushion around the nail's point and the timber.

2. Tap the head of the nail gently but firmly. It helps if you line the hammer and nail head up by looking straight down the shaft of the nail as if it were an arrow.

3. When the nail feels securely caught by the timber and unlikely to wobble, hit it home with a circular motion. Resist the temptation to tap, tap, tap directly down. Practise this a few times and you'll soon get the hang of it.

BASIC DRILLING AND SCREWING

There is a whole subspecies of horror films that takes delight in the power tool's potential to maim. Electric drills are no exception, so be extra vigilant and be careful where you drill.

1. Always ensure your body is fully behind the drill. This will not only help to keep it steady as it drills but will also allow you a nice clear view of what you're drilling.

2. When you've drilled what you want to drill, don't take your finger off the button since you'll find it a difficult and messy task removing a drill if it's not still drilling.

3. As with drilling, so with screwing. Hold the screw firmly in place, ensuring it goes into the wood without wobbling around.

BASIC SAWING

Sawing always looks far more heroic and strenuous than it actually is. Having said this, there is a knack to it – a knack that practice helps with and patience perfects.

1. Rather excitingly the handle of this saw and the untoothed edge create a perfect right angle, making it easy to mark out with a pencil a true line to follow.

2. Ensure the object to be sawn is placed on a secure, wobble-free surface onto which you can also (preferably) place a steadying knee. Keep your fingers away to the side and slowly draw the teeth of the saw over the marked edge.

3. Slowly and rhythmically draw the saw up, before allowing gravity to pull it down as much as possible. Pushing too much weight or over-pressing the down stroke will force the saw blade to bend, making sawing very heavy going.

TENON SAWING

For narrow, delicate or decorate mouldings or for when you need to cut a mitre joint, the tenon saw in a sawing box has a delicate finesse.

1. Line up the measured and marked-up moulding with the saw gap in the sawing box.

2. The tenon saw works properly only when it's kept completely horizontal, so resist the temptation to raise the handle as the teeth pass over the moulding.

3. For really delicate little mouldings, place a scrap of timber at the bottom of the sawing box to raise it up to a practical level for the cutting teeth of the tenon saw. This will also make it less easy to splinter the moulding as you saw.

BASIC JIG SAWING

The jig saw opens up a whole new horizon of shape sawing, but be very careful when operating it as this is one extremely dangerous piece of DIY kit.

1. Mark out the shape you intend to create. My tip is to use quite a dark, soft pencil so you'll still be able to see the pencil mark clearly when the dust starts flying.

2. As you plan your cutting, start working out in your mind where it will be safe for you to stand, keeping a close eye on where the electric cables are going to be.

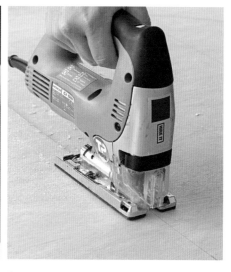

3. Make sure the saw is on a gentle setting rather than tree-felling turbo, and you're off! As with electric drills, electric saws must still be running when you remove them from the wood.

4. For practicality and safety's sake, circular shapes such as this should be drawn out as close as possible to the edge of the sheet of timber.

5. Ensure you keep your body, hands, fingers and extremities well behind the saw at all times. You may find that a steadying hand holding the two cut pieces together as you saw helps.

6. Little kinks or wobbles can be carefully removed after the main event.

DECORATIVE JIG SAWING

Creating a decorative shape from a sheet of timber is a wonderful way of finishing off a screen, mirror frame or bookcase. As a project its skill level is way below its considerable design impact.

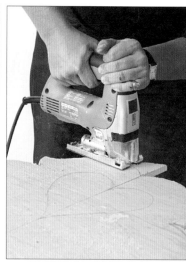

1. Start with a nice, straight line that will mark the centre of the symmetrical motif. Then draw one-half of whatever fancy pants, curly-wurly design you have in mind.

2. Now cut this shape out as carefully as possible, keeping it in one piece and finishing it along the straight edge of the centre line.

3. Now for the clever bit. Use the offcut from this first side as template for the other side by drawing around it in pencil. This should create a perfectly symmetrical mirror image.

4. Cut around the marked line on this second side as before, keeping a keen eye on safety.

5. For internal patterns like this heart, start the ball rolling with a nice thick drill bit. Drill down just inside the line to be cut.

6. You may find you need two, sometimes three, holes right next door to each other to create a large-enough slot for the jig saw's blade to fit into comfortably.

7. Starting from this drilled slot, saw out your shape. You may very well find you have to reposition the saw a bit in order to get around the shape in question.

8. Neaten up any clipped edges or missed turns with the jig saw set on a very slow speed before sanding the edges to finish.

SANDING

Believe it or not, there is a real art to sanding. Doing too little is worse than useless, but going over the top with a sandpaper that is that little bit too carnivorous can absolutely ruin a project.

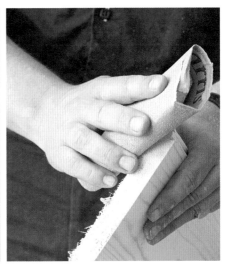

1. I always buy mixed packets of sandpaper. Coarse paper is great for butch, quick jobs but you'll need something finer for finessing. Whatever sheet you use, start by tearing it in half.

2. Always wrap your sandpaper around either a purpose-built, deliberately bought sanding block or a scrap of off-cut timber.

3. Wrapping the sandpaper around the block not only makes the whole process much less tiring but also, crucially, helps you to control what's going on.

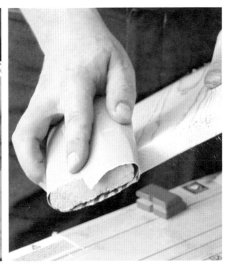

4. Use coarse paper initially to attack big bits of rough timber like this, turning the block every now and again so that the paper wears evenly.

5. Now switch to a finer paper to avoid losing the crisp edges of your saw cut to the over-abrasive attentions of heavier-grade papers.

6. As a final touch, gently and evenly smooth the edges off with the finest grade imaginable until it's all as smooth as a cherub's behind.

TONGUE-AND-GROOVE PANELLING

While some DIY 'experts' might tell you that you need to fix tongue-and-groove panelling with batons, I've always found sticking it works just as well. It also means you can put it straight down onto an existing skirting.

1. To start, you'll need a straight line to follow. Use a spirit level to give you both a vertical for the first plank and a horizontal for the heigh of each subsequent plank.

2. Apply a generous squiggle of panel adhesive. You'll find plenty of strong, sticky tubes on planet DIY that insist they'd stick your panels, architraves or mouldings up.

3. Though it's the adhesive that will hold up the planks for posterity, a little panel pin thumped through the plank into the plaster will stop any nasty sagging whilst this dries. (Sagging is always bad.)

4. Then - on your marks, get set, GO! See how fast you can get right the way around the room. But do make sure as you gothat every plank you attach is the same way around as its predecessor.

5. Finish the whole thing off with a moulding. Chances are you could stick it on but, as it might get knocked, I suggest screwing it in place.

6. Mark out where you want to put your screws using your spirit level to ensure that they are level.

7. Now drill through the moulding and into the wall. Don't forget to keep the drill turning as you draw it out.

8. Pop in a rawplug using a willing hammer, and screw the moulding to the wall. A diligent carpenter would use a countersink bit when drilling the hole into the moulding so that the screw head doesn't protrude.

WOOD PANEL MOULDINGS

There's nothing more gracious, elegant or jaw dropping-ly Georgian than a wall enhanced with regularly spaced mouldings. It's nothing like as hard to do as you'd think and if you use a light weight moulding that's not too ornate you can stick it and pin it in place without using screws.

1. Measure the length of your panel moulding and remember to mark which side of the measured line you'll be cutting your mitre.

2. Cut the mitre using a tenon saw and mitre block. Cut the mitre on top of a bit of scrap timber to hold it in place and stop it splintering as you finish sawing.

3. Mark out your panel on the wall using a spirit level.

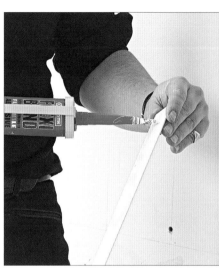

4. Apply a liberal squiggle of panel adhesive right the way down the moulding, making sure to keep the edges reasonably free of anything that might squelch out.

5. Now dull the panel pins you will be using to keep the moulding in place whilst the adhesive dries. Hit the sharp end gently to remove the sharpness from the point.

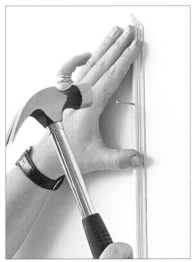

6. As you hammer the pin into the moulding you'll find that by dulling the pin you substantially reduce the chance of the panel moulding splitting along the line of the pin hole. It really does work, honest.

7. Before fixing the mouldings to the wall, lightly sand each mitre using fine braid sand paper. This will smarten up the join and get rid of any furry, splintery edges.

8. Continue panelling around the wall until the finished effect begins to resemble a very grand room in a very grand house.

HANGING A PICTURE

There's a simple rule to hanging pictures; make sure that the start of the top third of the picture is on exactly the same level as your eye. This is an infallible way of getting the height of pictures right.

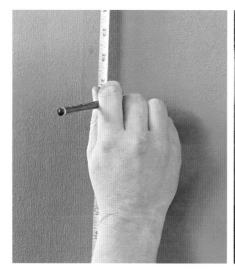

1. Having held the picture up to the wall and decided on its best position, measure out where you want the top of the picture frame to be.

2. Now measure the distance between the top of the picture and the taut picture wire as it will be once the picture is hung.

3. Use a picture hook at the point where you've subtracted the distance of the picture wire from the top of the picture.

HANGING A MIRROR

Mirrors are surprisingly heavy beasts which (since I'm sure there are few of you who would welcome seven years' bad luck) are worth fixing properly.

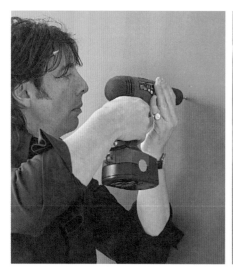

1. First of all check that there is no possibility of electrical cables under the plaster where you want to drill by avoiding areas around sockets and plugs.

2. Once you have marked your position and drilled into the wall, attach a rawplug and a screw long enough to protrude slightly from the wall once fully screwed in.

3. Hang the mirror on the protruding screw. Be gentle and patient, since not getting the wire onto the screw properly could lead to disaster.

HANGING A PICTURE WITH A MIRROR PLATE

I like to use mirror plates on ornate frames as they ensure the picture sits flat against a wall. They're also very useful for hanging pictures or mirrors on doors.

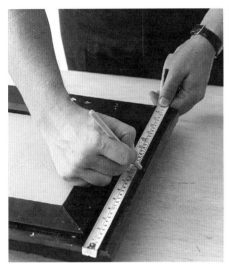

1. Find the midpoint of the picture frame and clearly mark it on the back with a pencil.

2. Hold the mirror plate in place so that its centre point corresponds with the mid mark of the frame.

3. Now use a bradawl to mark out a pair of holes in the timber that correspond with the holes on the mirror plate.

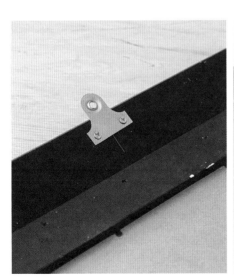

4. Screw the mirror plate to the back of the frame.

5. Position the picture where you intend to hang it, mark it through the hanging hole of the mirror plate before drilling and fixing a rawplug. Finish with a screw through the hanging hole.

6. On a door like this, rather than drilling, you will probably find that a bradawl will be sufficient to create a hole for the screw.

INSTALLING A BRACKET SHELF

Putting up a shelf is, believe me, satisfying beyond measure. To be able to arrange a few objects on a shelf that you are entirely responsible for takes house pride to a new level.

1. Firstly measure the shelf and work out where you want the brackets to be, before giving yourself a nice, level line to follow courtesy of a spirit level.

2. Finalise the position of the brackets and mark out a level vertical line which will correspond with the exact centre of the bracket. Offer the bracket up to the wall, lining it up between the vertical and horizontal lines, then use a pencil to mark the position of the screw holes.

3. Drill the marked holes using a drill bit slightly thicker than, but not longer than, the screws. Don't forget to keep the drill spinning as you take it out.

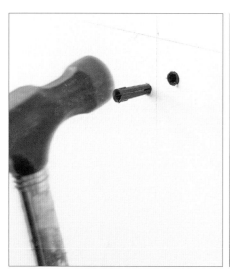

4. Pop rawlplugs into the holes and use some 'tough love' hammering to push them fully in.

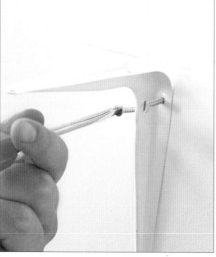

5. Hold up your shelf bracket and screw through the holes and into the rawlplugs behind.

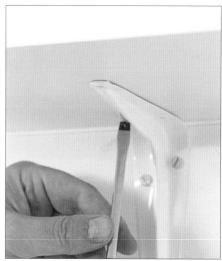

6. To keep the shelf steady, use the holes on the underside of the shelf's support bracket to drill and screw the bracket and shelf together.

INSTALLING A FLOATING SHELF

Shelves that seem to float on a wall have become extremely popular, with floating shelf kits now available pretty much everywhere. I am one of their most ardent fans, but remember – if you are thinking of installing these shelves, be careful not to overload them...or else.

1. Starting off with the assistance of your ever-helpful spirit level, mark out both a horizontal line the length of the shelf as well as a vertical line where you intend the centre of the shelf to be.

2. Offer up the (soon to be) concealed bracket to the wall and mark the exact position of the screw holes with a pencil.

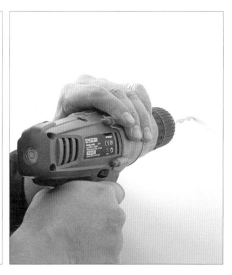

3. Follow the screw hole marks with a drill – ensuring you keep your bodyweight evenly behind it and your eyeline down the bit to create a nice, straight hole.

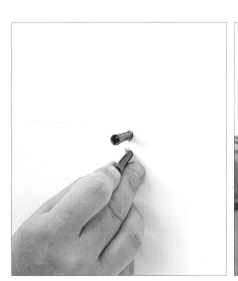

4. Now use rawlplugs to fill the hole. In desperation I've sometimes found myself using spent matches to do the rawlplugs job. While I wouldn't recommend them as a first choice, they do make for an acceptable substitute.

5. Screw the bracket into place. It's no bad thing to keep checking this with a spirit level as you go along, just to ensure that it is still nice and level.

6. Slide the floating shelf itself onto the prongs of the bracket. Many shelf kits also provide discreet screw holes on the underside so that the shelf can be firmly screwed to the concealed bracket.

FLOORING

LAYING LAMINATE FLOORING

When it first hit the scene, laminate flooring was responsible for a decorating revolution. It's easy to see why, as it enables you to easily achieve a wood (or more often wood effect) floor without the protracted hassle of sanding.

1. This floor is going straight onto a chipboard surface common in most modern houses. If you have old floorboards or an uneven surface it would pay to nail hardboard on top before you start.

2. The concealed nail principle of laminate flooring will ensure a seamless finish. Lay the first run of floor next to the skirting, nailing a panel pin through the tongue of each laminate board as you go. This will help hold the whole thing in place.

3. It's often a good idea to 'dull' the end of the panel pin by hitting the pointed end with a hammer before use, so that it won't split the wood.

4. Then start slotting the next boards together, making certain that the tongues and grooves of the planks fit together firmly as you go.

5. You may find that as you work your way around the room some boards prove difficult to fit together. If this is the case, try changing the board or switching ends around until they do.

6. Every two or three boards, give the whole thing a firm tap to ensure a nice tight fit. Use a block of timber as the battering ram and a hammer as the motivation. Never use a hammer on its own, as it'll almost certainly split the tongue or groove it hits.

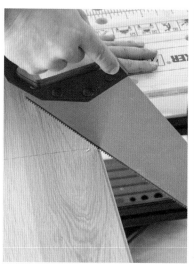

7. Should you need to, you'll be pleased to know that cutting laminate floor to size is satisfyingly easy. Always be very gentle as you start sawing, drawing the teeth of the saw respectfully over the fragile tongue.

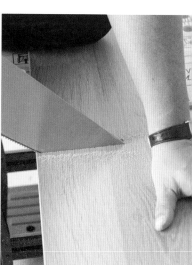

8. Support the sawn piece with a helping hand to ensure the laminate doesn't split itself when the two pieces separate as you finish sawing.

LAYING VINYL TILES

Shiny floors are a designer's trick for bouncing back light into dark rooms or corridors, and vinyl tiles are perfect for the job. They're easy to lay and fabulously easy to cut, making them the perfect flooring to accommodate odd-shaped floor layouts.

1. Vinyl tiles must be laid onto a completely flat, stable surface. They love concrete floors or chipboard floors but anything else such as floorboards will have to be evened off with a layer of chipboard before you begin.

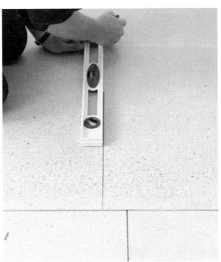

2. Before you begin laying your tiles, mark out a centre line onto your prepared surface from which your tile layout will start. Make sure that your centre line, as here, is visible and can't be mistaken for a join in the subfloor.

3. Now lay your tiles out in whatever pattern you have decided upon. Here I have opted for a chequerboard pattern of contrasting black and white tiles.

4. When you get to an edge that requires a tile to be cut to fit, place it under the tile next to it and mark a line to show where the cut needs to be made, before cutting with a sharp craft knife and a steel right angle.

5. Adhesive-backed tiles fly down provided the surface you want them to stick to isn't messy or dusty. Peel back the backing and just get on with it.

6. If your tiles aren't adhesive-backed and need glue, spread floor tile adhesive in evenly distributed, roughly metre-ish squares. The glue must not be so uneven as to affect the surface of the tiles and prevent a crisp, clean finish.

LAYING CARPET TILES

There has been a real, and encouraging, upswing in the popularity of carpet tiles of late, as designers have started creating products that look every bit the part in the home, rather than the office.

1. Make yourself a nice, straight centre line in the middle of the room for you to follow.

2. Now take the first of your flooring tiles and measure its centre line too.

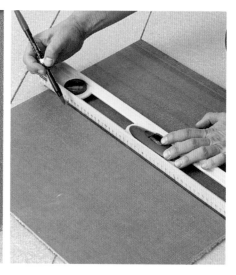

3. Mark the line clearly using a pen.

4. If your carpet tiles are not adhesive-backed, attach double-sided flooring tape to the edges on the back of the tile.

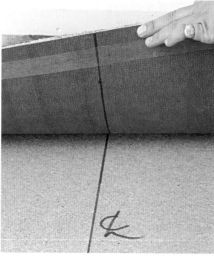

5. All carpet tiles have an arrow pointed on the reverse to show you which way the pile or pattern falls. Make sure as you go that the arrows on each tile point in the same direction.

6. Keep the pressure up and use the flats of your hands to make sure the joins between each tile are as tight and discreet as possible.

FLAMING AND STAINING FLOORBOARDS

Traditional floors always had a deep, lustrous finish that their proud owners hoped might be mistaken for French polishing. Here is my way of achieving the same effect with new wood boards. But remember, be careful now!

1. On new or recently restored boards, the best way to bring out that old, much-walked-on look is to singe the grain with a hand-held blowtorch.

2. Follow the safety instructions on your blowtorch carefully. Once lit, guide the flame across your wooden surface.

3. Use gentle sweeping motions to avoid creating lumpy burned welts on the surface of the grain.

4. Singe the floor slowly and gently, going lightly over areas again and again. You may find the odd blob of sap in the wood fizzles or stray splinter combusts – but don't panic.

5. At the edges, protect the wall with a fire-retardant board, which you will find on the shelves of a local plumbers merchant.

6. Remove lose carbonised wood, before bringing out the grain with a stout rubbing down using a fine brush.

7. Now apply your wood stain. I find that several coats always provide a wonderfully rich finish that shows off both the colour of the timber and its grain.

8. Finally apply a few coats of acrylic floor lacquer. You'll find the first coat goes on slowly, seems to get sucked up quickly and looks blotchy when dry. Don't fear – further coats will even out and intensify the effect.

COLOURWASHING FLOORBOARDS

Treating newly installed or recently refurbished floorboards to a spring-fresh colourwash is a classic Scandinavian decorating technique.

1. Start by getting your floorboards nice and wet, applying water with a large sponge. The wetter the floorboards are, the more open the grain will become, allowing the colourwash to penetrate nice and deep.

2. Alternate wiping the floorboards with your wet sponge with a going over with a wire brush to create a soggy, abraded surface that will be at its most receptive to the paint.

3. Personally, I tend not to use specially formulated colour washes as I find that standard white emulsions straight from the tin and rubbed into the grain work wonderfully.

4. Confine yourself to manageable metre-ish square blocks. This allows you to concentrate on getting one area right, before moving on to the next prepared area.

5. When dry, if you find that the colour isn't quite as dense as you would like, then repeat the process until you have achieved the desired look.

6. Finally, use a clear acrylic floor varnish over the top to finish. The traditional solution is to wax the coloured boards, but I find varnish quicker, more reliable and less prone to yellowing the finished effect.

STAINING A BORDER

Inlaid borders of different coloured timbers are a real motif of gracious French decorating. For those with a timber floor who find themselves embarrassed by a lack of luxurious inlay, the following technique is ideally suited.

1. Check the floor for protruding nail heads or other obstructions that might damage your floor sander. Sand the floor, going over it diagonally at first before finishing along the boards.

2. Now mark out the border that you are intending on staining, using a straight edge and a pencil.

3. With a craft knife, follow both the inside and outside lines of where the border needs to go. This is essential. The knife cuts the grain of the wood which prevents the woodstain, when applied, from travelling along the grain and looking horribly messy.

4. Apply masking tape around the edges of your border to avoid any unpleasant overspill of varnish.

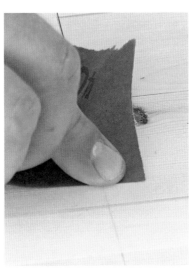

5. Use a craft knife to cut the internal corners clear of any stray bits of masking tape.

6. It's very important to remove any pencil marks from the area about to be stained before the woodstain seals them in for posterity. Sandpaper is the best tool to use for this.

7. Now apply the stain without the masked lines, brushing it in the direction of the grain. Apply coat after coat until you are happy with the stain effect.

8. To finish, carefully remove the masking tape. You'll see that the stain has been stopped in its tracks where the grain has been cut by the craft knife.

STENCILLING ONTO COLOURWASHED FLOORBOARDS

Finding a rug to suit a scheme can be a real hassle, so for an economical and highly personal solution I'll often advocate stencilling your own design.

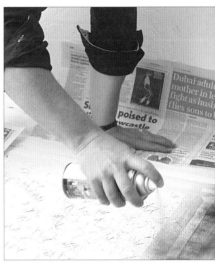

1. Colourwash the floor (see p208) for a nice bright background. Place the stencil and fix it where needed with non-permanent spray adhesive. Secure the edges firmly in place with masking tape.

2. If you want to create a border around your stencil, simply stick down another evenly spaced layer of masking tape around the outside of your motif.

3. Make sure that the floor outside the line of the tape is extremely well protected with plenty of newspaper that has been firmly stuck down.

4. Use spray enamel to stencil both the rug and border. I like to use spray enamel as it is extremely tough and will endure well without needing a further top coating of varnish. Spray painting is also less likely to stress or damage the stencil than painting with a brush or roller.

5. Open windows and wear a mask as you spray to keep the space well ventilated. Use short, gentle bursts of spray rather than long, heavy-duty ones.

6. Leave the spray to dry off. This only takes a few minutes. Then gently remove the newspaper and masking tape.

7. Carefully peel back the stencil to reveal the grand, extremely coordinated effect.

8. Should you want to experiment, try using different colours or using a variety of stencils to achieve an unlimited number of looks.

MAKING A CARPET WELL

This technique – the creation of a well within a wooden border in which a carpet may be stretched – is a perennial favourite of mine for tailored, elegant schemes.

1. Mark out where you want your carpet well on your underfloor. Now lay your floorboards (as here) or laminate flooring as normal, leaving the space that you have set aside for the carpet well bare.

2. If you are using floorboards, ensure that they are securely fixed with nails in neat rows.

3. Install carpet gripper rod to the internal edge of your carpet well. This is fearfully devilish stuff with a real penchant for pricking lax fingers, so be sure to be careful.

4. Cut your carpet piece to size before laying it within the wooden border. Rather than working your way around, I find it works best to work opposite sides – getting one side sorted before immediately heading over to the opposite side.

5. Carefully coax the raw edge of the carpet onto the waiting sharp teeth of the gripper rods.

6. Finally use your whole bodyweight to really push the carpet home, impaling the edges onto the gripper rod and making sure it's a nice, tight fit.

SOFT FURNISHING

COVERING A SCREEN

Soft furnishings bring comfort and interest to an interior and this simple yet highly effective technique makes for the perfect weekend afternoon project. For this particular job I like to use artist's canvas stretchers, which are available from art shops. They come in many different sizes and make the perfect frame for a folding screen or fabric panel.

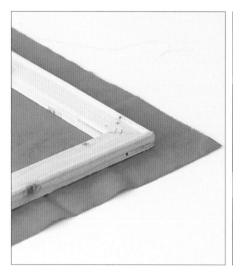

1. Start by cutting your fabric to size before laying it the wrong way round on a flat surface. Now place your chosen artist's canvas stretcher on top.

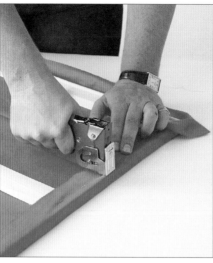

2. To avoid wrinkles or puckers in your fabric, getting the tension right is important. Stretch the fabric tightly around the stretcher before stapling it in the middle of the frame.

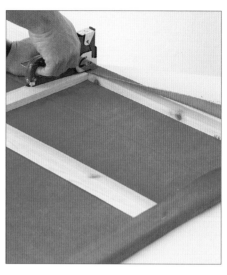

3. Now staple the opposite side. This keeps the fabric pulled equally. Finish by stapling the fabric onto the remaining two sides of your frame.

4. At corners, staple the fabric straight into the join before folding the adjacent piece of fabric into a triangle as neatly as you can.

5. Staple through the corner and make sure to remember the exact choreography of fold used on the first corner. Repeat as before on the remaining three corners.

6. There you have it – a simple panel. If you want to get a bit more advanced, try making a few further panels before fixing them together with a piano hinge or two to make a folding screen.

COVERING A CHAIR PAD

For me there's no point in being able to decorate a room unless you can finish it and finish it properly. Obviously reupholstering a large family sofa is a truly specialist task, but re-covering the pad of a dining chair is extremely easy and looks wonderful when done.

1. Pop the pad from the dining chair and cut the fabric to size. Allow a generous overhang all the way around to accommodate the rise of the pad's upholstery.

2. As with the screen, attach the fabric using a staple gun with one staple bang in the middle of each side. Always work from the opposite side to opposite side.

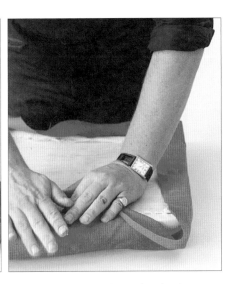

3. When fixed at the midpoint of each side, start stapling from middle out towards each corner, pulling the fabric tightly over the pad.

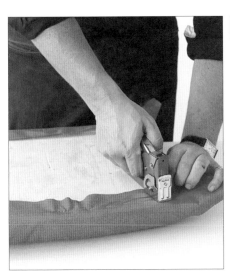

4. Try to keep the corners as neat as possible. But to be honest, once the pad is in the chair, the finished effect will be more than impressive enough to hide any small defects.

5. Fabrics that have a slight bit of stretch to them are perfect for this project and will make a nice, neat finish so much easier.

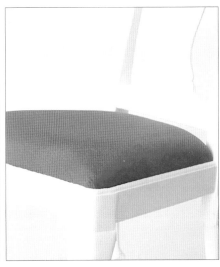

6. All that remains is to place your pad back in the chair, step back and admire your handywork.

UPHOLSTERING A HEADBOARD

Modern beds can be distinctly lacking in voluptuous drama, so why not try adding a generously upholstered headboard to impart exactly the right balance of soft comfort glamour.

1. Using a jig saw, cut yourself a basic headboard shape from plywood. When the shape is cut, use it as a template to draw around onto a piece of foam bought from a specialist foam shop.

2. Cut the foam to shape with a sharp knife. Several upholsterer friends of mine actually swear by bread knives to cut through foam or even electric carving knives to get through the really thick stuff.

3. Apply permanent spray adhesive or specialist foam adhesive generously onto your cut out foam. As foam is so absorbent you'll find you need several layers.

4. Stick the foam and shaped backboard together, then lay them face down onto the fabric you wish to use as upholstery.

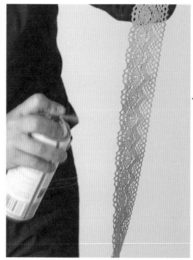

5. Staple the fabric onto the reverse of the backboard, starting in the middle of each side, then fixing its opposite before working around the rest of the headboard.

6. Pay particular attention to corners, keeping the tension on the fabric tight and the pressure up as you staple.
I find a few fiddles and practices are essential before I find a final solution.

7. A broad, decorative trimming like lace or a thick cord is a wonderful way of finishing it off as well as a great opportunity to cover up any little mistakes.

8. Permanent spray adhesives or specialist spray fabric glues are ideal for keeping edging and trimmings such as this in place.

MAKING A PELMET

Pelmets are perfect for finishing off curtains on an ugly pole or closing off the space above a blind. There was a time when pelmets were something of a dirty word, but now they're back with a vengeance.

1. Mark out your pelmet shape from some iron-on fabric interlining, before cutting it out. The fabric interlining will keep the pelmet nice and stiff.

2. Draw around the interlining onto your pelmet fabric, leaving a centimetre seam allowance.

3. Cut the fabric shape out, paying special attention to the extra that's been left for your seaming.

4. Iron the seams flat. Cut triangles out of the corners so that the seams can all be neatly ironed in.

5. As you come to each corner, hold the adjacent seam flat. This will ensure you don't iron out the seam you've just created.

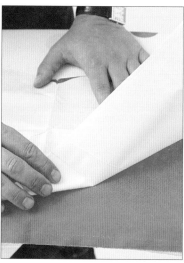

6. Place the iron on interlining face down onto the back of the fabric. It's the rather shiny, slightly adhesive side you'll want to put face down. Trim off any excess interlining.

7. Iron the back of the interlining. This will activate the glue and bind the lining and fabric together permanently.

8. Whilst it's all still warm and therefore not quite set, flip the pelmet over and iron out any unwanted creases from the front to finish.

MAKING A NO-SEW CURTAIN

A light, cheap and cheerful window dressing is more than possible without a sewing machine or a three-year university course in textiles - trust me.

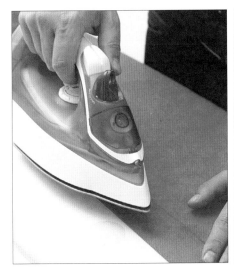

1. Measure, mark and cut out your chosen fabric to fit the window. Allow enough material for a generous seam at both sides as well as a good 20cm at both the top and the bottom.

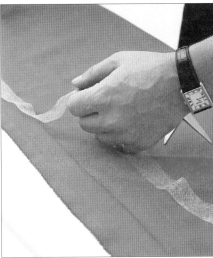

2. Now iron in your seams, giving them a nice crisp edge. This will make it easy to then apply iron-on hemming tape up to the edge of the fold.

3. Take time to ensure there are no folds or breaks in the tape and that the seam is completely finished. Don't attempt to install more than a metre at a time.

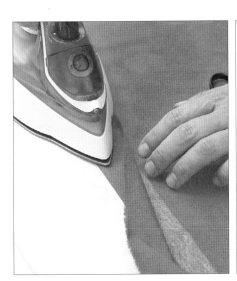

4. Now re-iron the seam, ensuring the fabric and tape fuse permanently together in the iron's heat.

5. At the top of the curtain, create a pocket for the curtain pole by folding over the 20cm sleeve before fixing iron-on hemming tape under its lower edge.

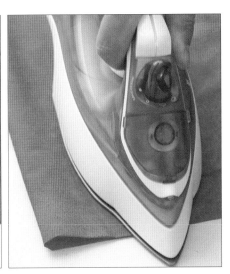

6. Iron firmly and flatly. You'll find simple pocket curtains like these are extremely easy to make as well as being a very useful way of finishing off a scheme.

INSTALLING A ROLLER BLIND

As a quick, easy and very modern window treatment, roller blinds are hard to beat. Roller blind kits are now widely available and come complete with extremely easy-to-install instructions.

1. Measure the area above your window accurately, making sure you've got an exact dimension for the width of the blind.

2. Measure the blind and, if necessary, follow the manufacturer's guidelines to cut it down to size.

3. Using the screws supplied and a screwdriver, install the end brackets directly into the window frame.

4. Pop the blind into the brackets. Pay particular attention to the winding mechanism which will be at one end, as it's very easy to put this in upside down.

HANGING A CURTAIN

Curtain poles can often be a furnishing statement in their own right. Choose one to complement a scheme or to carry through a design theme.

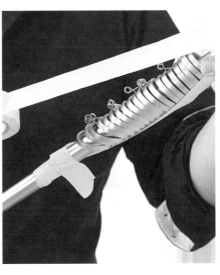

1. If your window frames aren't deep enough to screw in the curtain pole brackets directly, attach a 10cm piece of timber to the wall above using rawlplugs and screws as if it were an architrave.

2. Now screw the curtain pole brackets straight into the timber.

3. To stop the curtain rings sliding around (or indeed sliding off) in transit, I always stick them together with masking tape whilst I install the pole.

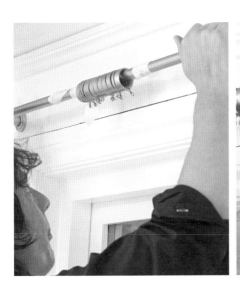

4. Pop the pole through the waiting support brackets. It'll be as you juggle the pole through one bracket then the other that you'll thank me for suggesting you fix the curtain rings in place.

5. Make sure there's one ring in the outside of the support bracket. This means the outside edge of the curtains will be held in place when they are pulled shut.

6. Finish by attaching the curtain to the rings using curtain hooks. Make sure that there are the same amount of curtain hooks in the curtain as there are rings in the pole.

GESSO WASH

It's so important to make a scheme feel loved and lived in by filling it full of bits and pieces that give it a homely touch. Gessso washing is a traditional and very elegant technique for softening down a harsh gold finish and achieving an aged look.

1. Start by mixing acrylic varnish with several spoonfuls of powder filler.

2. Paint the solution onto your gilded finish, ensuring it blobs and fills up areas of low relief.

3. Before the varnish dries fully, use a soft rag to wipe the gesso wash off the top edges of the gilded mouldings.

ANTIQUING WASH

Sometimes things just look a little too modern. Giving objects an aged look or a little bit of romantic history is one way of imbuing them with extra character and charm.

1. To create your antiquing wash, mixing brown and blue acrylic paint until they become a very sludgy non-colour – neither brown nor blue.

2. To this unattractive 'gravy', add acrylic varnish until it becomes thick, glossy and ever so slightly see-through.

3. With a smallish brush, rub the mixture over the surface you want antiqued. Pay particular attention to areas where age and dirt would build up, and apply lightly over edges or corners that would be rubbed and worn.

GOLD LEAFING

Covering precious objects in gold leaf was a real breakthrough for our ancient forbears. If you try the following technique, you'll discover how wonderful an experience it still is to take an ordinary object and make it gold.

1. Traditionally, gold leaf went onto gesso (a chalky primer) that had been tinted a rust colour with red oxide. Personally, I'm more than happy to suggest applying it onto red acrylic paint instead.

2. Cover the area to be gilded in acrylic gold size, which like PVA goes on white but dries clear. When it's gone clear, blot gold transfer leaf backed on disposable paper onto the sized surface.

3. Missing bits of gold or little excess flakes of leaf can be correctly repositioned with a dry brush. The idea is to use the leftover gold dust to fill in any bald patches.

FAKING WHITE GOLD LEAF

White gold leaf was always the cream of the gilding crop. Hollywood divas loved its luxurious glamorous modernity. Needless to day the real thing costs an arm and a leg but it can be faked...

1. White gold leaf has a characteristic warmth to it, so start off by spraying your object a startling, almost brassy gold. Then spray generously with permanent spray adhesive.

2. Now gently coax loose aluminium leaf (which isn't difficult to track down or expensive to buy) to stick to the sprayed surface with a stiff, dry brush.

3. Use a scalpel to flick off any stray bits or neaten up any ragged edges before encouraging all the little bits of leftover leaf to fill in any gaps with a dry paint brush.

DECOUPAGE

Decoupage is really just an extraordinarily frilly way of cutting and sticking. Victorian ladies loved to use this particular technique as a way of cheering up their screens or hat boxes.

1. Pick your motifs. Here extremely old-fashioned coloured engravings of traditional roses have been scanned from the computer onto heavy-duty copy paper.

2. When cut out, liberally apply a coat of PVA adhesive to the back of your desired motif. Ensure that the adhesive makes its way right to motif's edges.

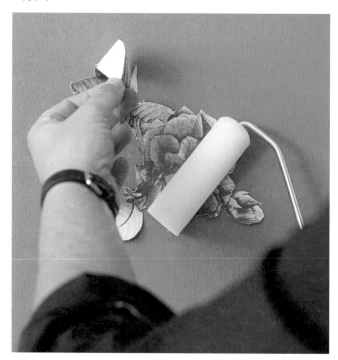

3. I always find a clean, dry foam roller to be ideal for sticking the cut shapes onto your surface. Start with pressure in the middle of your motif before working your way out to the edges.

4. If you want to intensify the effect, then create a repeat using additional images as here. If you are applying your motif to furniture, finish it by going over with a few coats of a hard-wearing varnish to ensure durability.

'GOLD LEAF' LINING

The Georgians loved to outline painted or lacquered furniture with an elegant line of gold leaf. I've discovered the perfect low-budget, low-tech way of faking it - a gold marker pen.

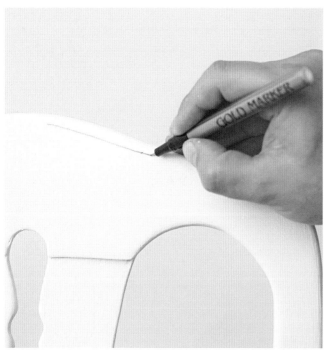

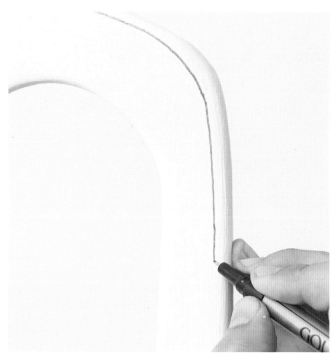

1. If you are applying your gold line to a flat, geometrically unchallenging surface then use a ruler to create a nice, crisp line. For something with a bit of curve to it, use the ring finger of your drawing hand as a guide to follow the shape.

2. Continue your line around the object, touching up any areas that need it as you go.

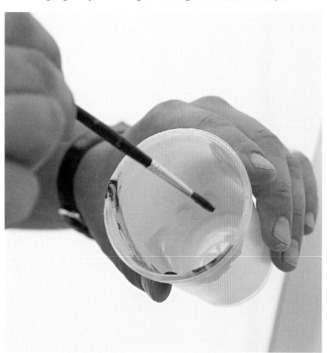

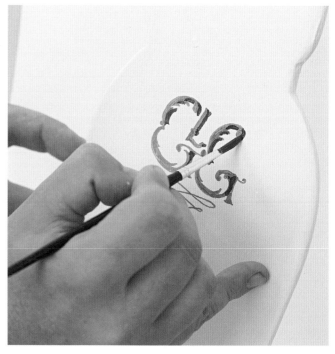

3. For an extra-special antiqued finish, mix up a very small amount of antiquing wash (see page 226).

4. This can then be applied to darken areas that you have already marked out with the gold pen to give the finished effect some depth and volume. Traditionally this is known as 'tole work'.

MAKING A SHELL MIRROR FRAME

Shells played a very important part in the history of classical Renaissance and Baroque design. I fell in love with the shell frame designed by Sophy Topley featured in 'From lowly to lovely' (see pages 100-103) that I thought I would have a go at making something similar myself. You know what they say about imitation being the sincerest form of flattery...

1. Using a really very ordinary flat mirror frame in unpainted timber, set out your collection of holiday shells, draw around them with a pencil when you're happy with their positioning.

2. Using heavy-duty panel adhesive, fill the hollows of each shell to be stuck.

3. Now, using the outlines as a guide, apply generous blobs of adhesive wherever the shells are to be placed. Place the shells on the frame.

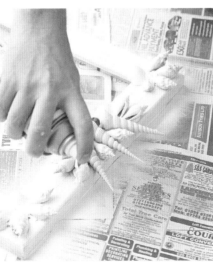

4. Give the adhesive a good 24 hours to really set solid before moving the frame onto a generous covering of newspaper. Wearing a mask, spray the mirror frame your desired colour using craft spray paint.

5. If you wanted to retain a little of the colour and finish of the shells, then you could try applying a gesso wash to them (see page 226). If not, then continue spraying in short, even bursts.

6. You may find you need to hold the mirror frame upright to make sure that you get into all the little spaces behind the shells.

COVERING A LAMPSHADE WITH WALLPAPER

I don't know why people resign themselves to lampshades that have nothing to recommend them save their neutrality and shading ability. I love lampshades that bring pattern, colour and luminosity to a room, and this is an easy way of making a boring lampshade do just that.

1. Start by spraying the inside of your lampshade gold. Gold inside the shade will create a wonderful warmth when the bulb is turned on.

2. When the gold is dry, stick several sheets of newspaper together to make one large piece that can comfortably cover the whole shade.

3. Fix the piece of newspaper in place, before trimming off the excess from the top and bottom with a pair of scissors.

4. When unwrapped you'll find yourself with a perfectly sized template that is ready for use.

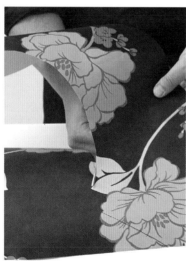

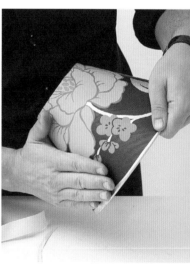

5. Use the template to mark out the wallpaper you want to cover the shade in. Remember to make sure you've placed the pattern where you want it to be seen.

6. Now cut the wallpaper out. I like to cut just inside the line so the wallpaper finishes just a little short at the top and bottom of the finished shade.

7. Apply a length or two of double-sided tape to the lampshade and fix the wallpaper in place.

8. When sticking the wallpaper to the shade, try to keep a consistent gap at both top and bottom to avoid creating a wallpaper 'lip' which could be damaged or torn.

COVERING A LAMPSHADE WITH TISSUE PAPER

Good-quality, printed tissue paper can easily be stuck on to anything to make elegant patchworks. Using tissue papers with contrasting patterns makes for an appealing, patchwork effect that will imbue any lampshade with style and character.

1. Start by painting the outside of your lampshade with a suitably coloured acrylic paint. This will provide the backdrop for your tissue paper patterns.

2. Cut your different patterned tissue papers into strips approximately the height of the shade.

3. Using a medium-sized brush, apply a liberal coat of PVA adhesive to the shade, before sticking the tissue paper pieces onto it in relatively random order. Every so often use the brush to flatten the paper and apply more PVA to the surface.

4. When you have covered the lampshade completely in paper, cut the edges in a straight line about half a centimetre from the edge of the shade. Using PVA, encourage the paper to stick over the edge in a neat hem.

5. Finally, apply an additional top coat of PVA to the shade for a tough lacquer shine.

6. Patterned tissue paper can be coaxed over a variety of shaped surfaces (for added impact, why not try it on your lamp stand too) and can make even the most dull objects look quite special.

STOCKISTS

The following is a list of the various stockists responsible for making each of the 30 rooms featured within this book look as gorgeous as they do. Product ranges may change over time, so if you are intending on heading to a specific store I suggest you save yourself the possibility of a wasted journey by checking the products' availability on the relevant website in advance.

1: Baroque 'n' roll
Bedlinen: LLB 'Divine Decadance'; www.rectella.co.uk
Black candles: www.cargohomeshop.com
Carpet: Abbotsford border plaid; www.brintons.net
Curtain fabric: Finn gold; www.voyagedecoration.com
Gold beanbag: www.heals.co.uk
Gold candlesticks & cushions: www.homesense.com
Gold spray paint: www.plasti-kote.co.uk
Headboard: www.thefrenchfurniturecompany.co.uk
Mirror & gold clock: LLB Influence Collection; www.matalan.co.uk
Paint: Jack Black in Ultimatt emulsion; www.thelittlegreene.com
Postcards: www.tate.org.uk
Toy knights: www.papo-france.com, www.justschleich.co.uk, www.spmodels.co.uk
Valance around bed: Escama old gold; www.voyagedecoration.com
Wallcovering: Allure 07 Black; www.muraspec.com
Wallpaper: Bamboo Trellis in black & gold; www.thibautdesign.com

2: The wonder of one
Cushions, yellow plates & lime glass lamp: www.homesense.com
Fret cut screen: www.jali.co.uk
Pantone mugs: www.2products.com
Sunflower wall stickers: www.ficklestix.com

3: All natural ingredients
China hens & green leaf dishes: Moonstruck, Cirencester, England; 01285 640444
Green gnome candles & long green dishes: www.hihosilver.co.uk
Green round rug: glamour rug in grass; www.therugseller.co.uk
Lampshades: www.tkmaxx.com
Ornate columns, buckets, horn table lamps, wooden birds & wooden hearts: www.cowleyhouse.com
Wooden end cabinets: www.minerva-antiques.co.uk

4: Bath night at the opera
Bath (hand painted), basin & taps: www.heritagebathrooms.com
Candles: www.forlivingandgiving.com
Carpet: LLB manoir; www.brintons.net
Lamp base: www.tkmaxx.com
Screen: www.cowleyhouse.com
Wallpaper: Chantilly in black; LLB definitive collection; www.grahambrown.com

5: Living in the closet
BiOrb Life Aquariums: www.reef-one.com
Chairs: www.scumble-goosie.co.uk
Coffee table print & gloss digital print: digitalprint@typecraft.co.uk
Red rug, red kettle & red salt & pepper mills: www.homesense.com
Drums: www.qcmilitaria.com
Wall stencils (shields & crests): www.stencil-library.com

6: Contemporary cocoon
Assorted candelabras & cushions: www.tkmaxx.com
Floor lamps: www.dwell.co.uk
Metal detail room screen: Moonstruck, Cirencester, England; 01285 640444
Fur throws & cushions: www.matalan.co.uk
Sculpture: www.spellersculptures.com
Candles in candelabra: www.forlivingandgiving.com

7: Busy bathroom
Basin & taps: www.heritagebathrooms.com
Chalk paint pens: www.chalkpens.com, www.edding.com
Digital print blind: www.printedspace.com
Illustrations: D Shoosmith; www.dshoosmith.co.uk
Metal buckets: www.matalan.co.uk
Orange bath accessories: www.zarahome.com
Paint emulsion: Mid Lead & Shirting in Ultimatt emulsion; www.thelittlegreene.com
Snood Elaina cut out cylinder downlight: www.aimbry.co.uk
Towels: Missoni Home; available from www.amara.co.uk
Toiletries: www.thesanctuary.co.uk

8: A bon viveur bedroom
Cream bedlinen, copper vase & copper candlesticks: www.homesense.com
Fluffy cushion & copper bowl: www.heals.co.uk
Laser transfer for wine labels: www.fredaldous.co.uk
Metal wall sculpture: The Giltwood Gallery, Cheltenham, England; 01242 512540
Red glass lamp: www.chelsom.co.uk
Whisper Shiney shaggy rug in plum: www.therugseller.co.uk

9: Retro retrod
Chenille twist large brown rug: www.dwell.co.uk
Cushions: www.tkmaxx.com
Fabric on table: arkona collection; www.voyagedecoration.com
'Fern' picnicware: www.johnlewis.co.uk
Pots: www.lecreuset.co.uk
Striped cushion: www.cargohomeshop.com
Wallpaper pattern: Helsinki LLB definitive collection; www.grahambrown.com
Decorating by Decorating Solutions (07775995542)

10: Making an entrance
Bonaldo coat tree: www.heals.co.uk
Gloss white desk: www.dwell.co.uk
Karen Blixen white floor vase: www.95percentdanish.com
Light switches: www.focus-sb.co.uk
Pendant lights: le klint donut; www.skandium.com
Round white mirror: www.morrismirrors.com
Silver boots: www.hunter-boot.com
White flokati rug: www.therugseller.co.uk
White leather tub chair: www.dwell.co.uk

11: A secret lair with flair
Coloured glasses: LLB Fabulous Flutes; www.dartington.co.uk
Cushions: LLB Influence Collection; www.matalan.co.uk
Cutlery: www.arthurprice.co.uk
Furniture: www.gl50.co.uk
Plates, candlesticks & cushions: www.homesense.com
Sheepskin cushions: www.britishsheepskins.co.uk

12: Ultra violet
Black globe, white storage vases, chrome oil burners, ponyskin cube & star wall decorations: www.cowleyhouse.com
Black leather storage boxes: LLB Influence Collection; www.matalan.co.uk
Fabric for purple velvet throw: www.robertallendesign.com
Faux lavender: www.ruckley.com
Hand-made candles: www.parabledesigns.co.uk
Large purple rug (Ascot Elite Bramble): www.abbeymillcarpets.co.uk
Paint: Shirting in Ultimatt emulsion; dark lead colour in flat oil; www.thelittlegreene.com
Plain purple cushions & tealight holders: www.cargohomeshop.com
Purple 'feature' chair: www.anangelatmytable.co.uk
Purple glass lamp: www.chelsom.co.uk
Purple patterned cushions: www.next.co.uk
Purple velvet fabric: Astoria fabric; www.kestrel-lister.co.uk

Silver dish, silver 'teardrop' dishes & hurricane lamps: www.hihosilver.co.uk
Spotted black cushions & various picture frames: www.tkmaxx.com
'Twig' wall lights: www.vaughandesigns.com
Wallpapers: Mystique (on walls) & Navona (on coffee table)
LLB Definitive Collection; www.grahambrown.com
White mirrored art: Moonstruck, Cirencester, England; 01285 640444

13: Hero of the shower
Digital print of Venice on waterproof laminate: digitalprint@typecraft.co.uk
Flooring: Urban Metal Riven Marble; www.amtico.co.uk
Ianthe towels: www.liberty.co.uk
Peacock towels collection: LLB Influence Collection; www.matalan.co.uk
Silver & chrome stickers on shower panel: www.cotswoldsigncoltd.co.uk
'Snood' down lighters: www.aimbry.co.uk
Toothbrush holder & soap dispenser: www.matalan.co.uk
Various bath products: www.loccitane.co.uk
Wallpaper: www.osbourneandlittle.com
Winchester towel rail: www.heritagebathrooms.com

14: Knockout knock through
Carpet inserts: Carousel (83) kingfisher; www.yourfloors.co.uk
Coffee table & picture frames: www.cargohomeshop.com
Console table: www.dwell.co.uk
Curtain fabric: www.harlequinharris.com
Dining chairs: www.markelliot.co.uk
Door handles: www.chsironmongery.co.uk
Feature chairs & footstool: www.okadirect.com
Flooring: Balterio Tradition quartto laminate; www.yourfloors.co.uk
Paint: Linen wash & Joanna in Ultimatt emulsion; www.thelittlegreene.com
Pendant & floor lights: www.taylighting.com
Plinth: www.plinthsandpedestals.co.uk
Radiators: Ancona in mottled copper; www.theradiatorcompany.co.uk
Sculpture: www.thesculptureroom.co.uk
Sockets: Horizon sockets in antique brass; www.focus-sb.co.uk
Throw fabric: 'Shake' kingfisher; www.voyagedecoration.com
Vases, lamps, clock, bowls & cushions: www.tkmaxx.com
Wallpaper: Extravagance pattern no. 15372 elite; www.harlequin.uk.com
Curtain making by www.fabricmills.co.uk
Decorating by Decorating Solutions (07775995542)

15: Post-punk princess
Artwork: Kate Kessling; www.contrarypress.com & www.paulkessling.com
Black spray paint: www.plasti-kote.co.uk
Digital prints for frames: digitalprint@typecraft.co.uk
Guitar & amp: www.aroundaboutsound.co.uk
Lavazza print: www.lavazza.com
Lazer transfer for wall prints: www.fredaldous.co.uk
Mannequin: LLB Influence Collection; www.matalan.co.uk
Multi-coloured capiz shell chandelier: www.aimbry.net
Paint: Blue Verditer in Ultimatt emulsion; www.thelittlegreene.com
Pink fabrics: www.wilman.co.uk
Pink laser cut screen: www.jali.co.uk
Small mirrors on wall: www.charmedincornwall.co.uk
Wallpaper used as headboard: soho stripe 84/4016; www.cole-and-son.com
White frames for vinyl records: www.vinylart.co.uk
Zebra stencil for rug: www.stencil-library.com

16: Spring greens
Flutes: LLB Fabulous Flutes; www.dartington.co.uk
Plates & peacock pattern bowls: www.epicureaneurope.co.uk
Print for shades: www.digitalprint@typecraft.co.uk
Switches & sockets: www.focus-sb.co.uk
Trim for bobble fringe for lampshades: www.originalsbyalexia.co.uk
Wallpaper: Mystique LLB Definitive Collection; www.grahambrown.com
Worktop: www.pyrolave.co.uk

17: Surf shack sophisticate
Capiz shell light (outside): www.aimbry.co.uk
Cutlery: LLB Echo range; www.arthurprice.com

Dining table, benches & driftwood pieces: Arty Crafts, Wadebridge, England;
01208 812274
Fabric for chair & cushions: Tuska pink; www.malabar.co.uk
Floor light: www.okadirect.com
Globe lights: www.dwell.co.uk
Grey & white fringe curtain: www.cargohomeshop.com
Pebble carpet tiles: www.heuga.com
Pink bag: www.charmedincornwall.co.uk
Pink cutout table mats: www.homesense.com
Plants in planters: www.peonydirect.co.uk
Sofa: www.sofas.co.uk
Wire planters: www.deroma.com
White gloss spray paint (on gnomes): www.plasti-kote.co.uk
White leather bean bag: www.cozibag.co.uk
White shell candle holders, silk flowers & ceramic stool: Moonstruck, Cirencester;
England; 01285 640444
Upholstery by Andrew Reeves Upholstery (01242 221577)

18: Silver surfers' surface
Blue lamps & shades: www.tingewickpottery.co.uk
Cushions & glass square vases: www.tkmaxx.com
Fabric for curtains: quality 283 design: 11614/F5; Lovat Mill, Hardwick, Scotland;
01450 373231
Fabric for cushions: kirkton 584 & 583; Lovat Mill
Leather flooring tiles: colour 9012 tan; www.leatherflooring.co.uk
Paint: Sky Blue in Ultimatt emulsion; www.thelittlegreene.com
Pictures in collection on wall: www.hares-antiques.com
Various vases & ornaments: Giltwood Gallery, Cheltenham, England; 01242 512540
Wall covering: Jumeriah P8821; www.muraspec.com

19: Mrs de Winter wonderland
3-tier clear & black beaded pendant lights: www.aimbry.co.uk
Black fringe trim on curtains: www.britishtrimmings.com
Carpet: LLB Manoir; www.brintons.net
Curtains: www.fabricmills.co.uk
Large black wall-mounted mirror: www.matalan.co.uk
Trim on lampshade: 5025 fringe; www.wendycushing.com
Wallpaper: Taffetia LLB Collection in ruby & gold; www.grahambrown.com
Decorating by Decorating Solutions (07775995542)

20: From lowly to lovely
Bench, cushions & rug: www.lauraashley.com
Firescreen, pots & small urns: www.cowleyhouse.com
Floating shelves: www.diy.com
Flowers (silk): www.peonydirect.co.uk
Lamps: www.frenchgreyinteriors.co.uk
Large urns & coffee table: www.burford.co.uk
Paint: Chamois, Light Gold, Stone Pale Cool & Whitening in Ultimatt emulsion;
www.thelittlegreene.com
Plinths: www.plinthsandpedestals.co.uk
Paint effects: D Shoosmith; www.dshoosmith.co.uk
Radiator covers: www.jali.co.uk
Shell mirror above fire: Sophy Topley; www.sophytopley.co.uk

21: Net loft chic
Black lamps, large black mirror, Venetian mirror, leather draw units, large clock &
shaggy cushions: LLB Influence Collection; www.matalan.co.uk
Digital posters in living area: digitalprint@typecraft.co.uk
Kitchen taps: www.capability-online.co.uk
Paint: Gentle Sky, James & Sky Blue in Ultimatt emulsion, Juniper Ash in floor paint;
www.thelittlegreene.com
Stair ropes: www.stairropes.com
Decorating by Roy Speakman (0779602404)

22: Shopaholic heaven
Bench seat: www.lauraashley.com
Curtains: www.fabricmills.co.uk
Fabric for storage boxes: www.originalsbyalexia.co.uk
Flokati rug: www.therugseller.co.uk
Leather headboard: www.silcox.co.uk

Paint: Gauze & Mischief in Ultimatt emulsion; www.thelittlegreene.com
Shopping bags: www.beatricevontresckow.com
Silver cushions: www.heals.co.uk
Swivelling tub chair: www.dwell.co.uk
Wallpapers: Bird in the Bush & Bouquet patterns; www.annafrench.co.uk
Wave glass shade table lamp: www.dwell.co.uk
White gloss console table: www.dwell.co.uk
White mirror: Moonstruck, Cirencester, England; 01285 640444
White throw on bed & pink flock candlesticks: www.tkmaxx.com
Wire mannequin: Monday Trading Co., Cirencester; 01285 640100
Decorating by Decorating Solutions (07775995542)

23: Well-mannered manor
Carpet: LLB Rococco pattern; www.brintons.net
Curtains: www.fabricmills.co.uk
Decoupage on table: www.decopatch.com
Door handle: flush ring brass handle; www.chsironmongery.co.uk
Faux books in jib door & coral tie backs: www.originalbooks.net
Framing: www.thepictureframers.co.uk
Printed lampshades: digitalprint@typecraft.co.uk
Radiators: www.theradiatorcompany.co.uk
Smoked mirror panels: Tivoli Glass, Cheltenham, England; 01242 578732
Wallpaper: Jaisamand, LLB definitive collection; www.grahambrown.com
Sofa construction & upholstery by Andrew Reeves (01242 221577)
Panelling & bookcase construction by Andy Kent Construction (www.andykentconstruction.co.uk)

24: Pearly queen
Carpet: Costello CS/152; www.abbeymillcarpets.co.uk
Chandelier above bed, bedside lights, bedside tables, dressing table, dressing table stool, full-length mirror & floor lamps: www.rvastley.co.uk
Cornice: www.plastermouldingsonline.com
Curtains: www.fabricmills.co.uk
Fabric for chaise longue, curtains & pelmets: Villa Nova Vn 1190/18 Organza, Villa Nova 2027/Naples 'Nightshade' & Giselle 1018/ME Yukiko; www.voyagedecoration.com
Light switches: www.focus-sb.co.uk
Paint: China Clay in flat oil, Mid Lead colour & Secret Shell in acrylic matt, Welcome in Ultimatt emulsion & Whitening in acrylic matt; www.thelittlegreene.com
Radiator covers: www.jali.co.uk
Wall mural: D Shoosmith; www.dshoosmith.co.uk
Wall stencil: www.stencil-library.com
Wallpaper: L'Orient Elixir Stone Memo; SA eliwall-381-ME; www.voyagedecoration.com

25: Summer living had me a blast
Cutlery: LLB Meander range; www.arthurprice.com
Curtains: www.fabricmills.co.uk
Fabric for lampshades & curtains: Thibaut 'Spring Lake'; www.annafrench.co.uk
Glasses: LLB Ember range; www.dartington.co.uk
Glass top for dining table: Glass Act, Cirencester, England; 01285 656 977
Paint: Aquamarine in matt acrylic; www.thelittlegreene.com
Wallpaper: Thibaut Spring Lake; www.annafrench.co.uk
Decorating by Decorating Solutions (07775995542)

26: Rose room
Bedspreads: The Attic, Bocastle, Cornwall, England; 01840 779009
Curtains: www.nicolavickeyinteriors.co.uk
Cushions on chair: www.charmedincornwall.co.uk
Decopatch on chest of drawers, floor lamps & shades: www.decopatch.com
Mirror: LLB Influence Collection; www.matalan.co.uk
Paint: Baked Cherry in eggshell; www.thelittlegreene.com
Construction and decorating by Roy Speakman (07790602404)

27: Escaping the parent trap
Bedlinen & Hear Cushions: LLB collection; www.rectella.co.uk
Black bathroom tiles: www.firedearth.com
Carpet tiles: Lazy Lounge; www.heuga.co.uk
Cowshed lifestyle range: www.cowshedonline.com
Digital print blinds: www.printedspace.com
Digital print wall transfers: www.cotswoldsigncoltd.co.uk

Feature light above bed: Giltwood Gallery, Cheltenham, England 01242 512540
Heart cushions: LLB collection; www.rectella.co.uk
Picture frames, candlesticks & towels: www.homesense.com
Rabbit table lamp: www.foundryonline.co.uk
Spacehopper: www.tsttoys.com
Wall covering: Opulence Sequins 21; www.muraspec.co.uk
Wall lights in headboard: www.cto-lighting.co.uk
White gloss cabinet: www.dwell.co.uk
White leather fabric: Griffine Aquarius ivory; www.warwick.co.uk
Upholstery by Andrew Reeves Upholstery (01242 221577)

28: House guest heaven
Curtain & bed spread fabric: www.warwick.co.uk
Curtains & blinds: www.fabricmills.co.uk
Crystal decanters: Pickwick Antiques, Boscastle, Cornwall, England; 01840 250770
Cushions: www.johnlewis.com
Fret cut decorative panels: www.jali.co.uk
Wall lights: Armada Antiques, Cheltenham, England; 01242 529812
Upholstery by Andrew Reeves Upholstery (01242 221577)

29: The hallway gallery
Acrylic: www.theplasticshop.co.uk
Drum shades: www.aimbry.co.uk
Feature chair: www.pinkappledesigns.co.uk
Flooring: 'Lazylawn'; www.lazylawn.co.uk
Laser-cut acrylic panels: www.jali.co.uk
Printed covers for shades: digitalprint@typecraft.co.uk
White floor lamp: www.aimbry.co.uk
Wire 'cage' planters: www.deroma.co.uk

30: Tidy up time
Carpet tiles: www.rawsoncarpets.co.uk
Connaught wall lights: www.johnlewis.com
Fabric for seat cushions: Encore Mineral; www.villanova.co.uk
Fabric for throw on sofa: Sansai Sumi Riverside; www.warwick.co.uk
Fabric for cushions: melanie colour 8 & colour 68; www.annafrench.co.uk
Lampshades & cushions: www.tkmaxx.com
Radiator covers: www.jali.co.uk
Robot mugs & striped chairs: www.cowleyhouse.com
Square mirror: www.heals.co.uk
Striped cushions: www.cargohomeshop.com
Striped mural: D Shoosmith; www.dshoosmith.co.uk
Wooden storage unit & wooden letters: www.little-childs.co.uk

ACKNOWLEDGEMENTS

Thanks to Ed and Faye Bowen, Jon and Jules Silver, Tim and Zoe Bawtree, Kate and Paul Kessling, Mark and Donna Kraven, Steve and Davina Clift and Sean and Faye Hodgson. Thanks also to all at GL50 (www.gl50.co.uk), the Lower Mill Estate (www.lowermillestate.com), the Watermark Club (www.watermarkclub.co.uk), the Bay in Talland (www.thebaytalland) and to Ursula and the team at Urban Splash (www.urbansplash.co.uk).

Thanks also to Decorating Solutions (07775995542), Andy Kent Construction (www.andykentconstruction.co.uk), Andrew Reeves Upholstery (01242 221577), Fabric Mills (www.fabricmills.co.uk), Roy Speakman (07790602404) Travis Perkins and B&Q (www.diy.com) for their part in helping transform the rooms within these pages from ideas into reality.

INDEX